7th Workshop on Cognitive Modeling and Computational Linguistics (CMCL 2017)

Valencia, Spain
3 April 2017

ISBN: 978-1-5108-3861-1

Printed from e-media with permission by:

Curran Associates, Inc.
57 Morehouse Lane
Red Hook, NY 12571

Some format issues inherent in the e-media version may also appear in this print version.

Printed by Curran Associates, Inc. (2017)

Association for Computational Linguistics
209 N. Eighth Street
Stroudsburg, Pennsylvania 18360

Phone: 1-570-476-8006
Fax: 1-570-476-0860

acl@aclweb.org

Additional copies of this publication are available from:

Curran Associates, Inc.
57 Morehouse Lane
Red Hook, NY 12571 USA
Phone: 845-758-0400
Fax: 845-758-2633
Email: curran@proceedings.com
Web: www.proceedings.com

CMCL 2017

Cognitive Modeling and Computational Linguistics (CMCL 2017)

Proceedings of the 7th Workshop

EACL 2017 Workshop
April 3, 2017
Valencia, Spain

Thanks to our generous sponsors:

The Center for Cognitive and Brain Sciences at The Ohio State University

The Ohio State University Department of Linguistics

The Massachusetts Institute of Technology Department of Brain and Cognitive Sciences

Introduction

The seventh workshop in Cognitive Modelling and Computational Linguistics (CMCL 2017) was held in Valencia, Spain, alongside the annual meeting of the European chapter of the Association for Computational Linguistics (EACL 2017). This year's proceedings reflect the introduction of new methods in bridging computational linguistics and psycholinguistics, such as the neural models and deep learning techniques that have been sweeping other areas of computational linguistics. This year also saw the introduction of a new structure to CMCL, including a poster session, long and short paper tracks, and a non-archival abstract track. We invited two speakers this year, Prof. Anders Søgaard of the University of Copenhagen and Prof. Raquel Fernández of the University of Amsterdam, handed out a Best Student Paper Award, and gave travel grants to four student authors. We obtained sponsorship for awards, grants, and invited speaker costs via the Ohio State University Center for Cognitive and Brain Science, the Ohio State University Department of Linguistics, and the Massachusetts Institute of Technology Department of Brain and Cognitive Sciences.

This year, we received twenty paper submissions in total, of which two were eventually withdrawn. We accepted four papers as oral presentations, two as poster presentations with archival papers, three non-archival poster presentations, and one cross-submitted poster presentation. We would like to thank the authors, reviewers, and attendees for making this workshop a successful endeavour.

Ted Gibson
Tal Linzen
Asad Sayeed
Marten van Schijndel
William Schuler

Organizers

Ted Gibson, Massachusetts Institute of Technology
Tal Linzen, École Normale Supérieure
Asad Sayeed, Saarland University
Marten van Schijndel, The Ohio State University
William Schuler, The Ohio State University

Program Committee:

Omri Abend, Hebrew University of Jerusalem
Steven Abney, University of Michigan
Afra Alishahi, Tilburg University
Fatemeh Torabi Asr, Indiana University
Klinton Bicknell, Northwestern University
Christos Christodoulopoulos, University of Illinois at Urbana-Champaign
Alexander Clark, King's College
Matthew Crocker, Saarland University
Jennifer Culbertson, George Mason University
Vera Demberg, Saarland University
Brian Dillon, University of Massachusetts
Ewan Dunbar, LSCP
Micha Elsner, The Ohio State University
Afsaneh Fazly, University of Toronto
Naomi Feldman, University of Maryland, College Park
Michael C. Frank, Stanford University
Stefan Frank, Radboud University Nijmegen
Stella Frank, Edinburgh University
Alona Fyshe, University of Victoria
Sharon Goldwater, University of Edinburgh
Thomas Graf, Stony Brook University
John T. Hale, Cornell University
Keith Hall, Google
Tim Hunter, University of California, Los Angeles
Evan Jaffe, The Ohio State University
Frank Keller, University of Edinburgh
Shalom Lappin, University of Gothenburg
Roger Levy, Massachusetts Institute of Technology
Pavel Logacev, Bogazici University
Emily Morgan, Tufts University
Aida Nematzadeh, University of California, Berkeley
Timothy John O'Donnell, Massachusetts Institute of Technology
Sebastian Padó, University of Stuttgart
Bozena Pajak, Duolingo
John K. Pate, University of Buffalo
Roi Reichart, Technion University
David Reitter, Penn State University
Brian Roark, Google
Hinrich Schuetze, Ludwig Maximilian University of Munich
Ed Stabler, University of California, Los Angeles
Mark Steedman, University of Edinburgh

Shravan Vasishth, Potsdam University
Titus von der Malsburg, University of California, San Diego
Colin Wilson, Johns Hopkins University
Alessandra Zarcone, Saarland University
Jelle Zuidema, University of Amsterdam

Invited Speakers:

Raquel Fernández, University of Amsterdam (Netherlands)
Anders Søgaard, University of Copenhagen (Denmark)

Table of Contents

Conference Program

Monday, April 3, 2017

8:30–9:20 **Registration**

9:20–11:00 **Session 1**

9:20–9:30 ***Introductory remarks***

9:30–10:30 *Invited talk 1: Everytime I hire a penguin*
Anders Søgaard

10:30–11:00 *Entropy Reduction correlates with temporal lobe activity*
Matthew Nelson, Stanislas Dehaene, Christophe Pallier and John Hale

11:00–11:30 **Coffee break**

11:30–13:00 **Session 2**

11:30–12:00 *Learning an Input Filter for Argument Structure Acquisition*
Laurel Perkins, Naomi Feldman and Jeffrey Lidz

12:00–12:30 *Grounding sound change in ideal observer models of perception*
Zachary Burchill and T. Florian Jaeger

12:30–13:00 *"Oh, I've Heard That Before": Modelling Own-Dialect Bias After Perceptual Learning by Weighting Training Data*
Rachael Tatman

Monday, April 3, 2017 (continued)

13:00–14:30 Lunch

14:30–16:00 Poster session

Be Precise or Fuzzy: Learning the Meaning of Cardinals and Quantifiers from Vision
Sandro Pezzelle, Marco Marelli, and Raffaella Bernardi

"He's pregnant": simulating the confusing case of gender pronoun errors in L2 English
Chara Tsoukala, Stefan L. Frank, and Mirjam Broersma

Incremental generative model of sentence linearization and word order variation
Kristina Gulordava and Frank Keller

Inherent Biases of Recurrent Neural Networks for Phonological Assimilation and Dissimilation
Amanda Doucette

In search of the human-like predictability model
Anastasiya Lopukhina, Konstantin Lopukhin, and Anna Laurinavichyute

Predicting Japanese scrambling in the wild
Naho Orita

16:00–16:30 Coffee break

Monday, April 3, 2017 (continued)

16:30–18:00 Session 3

16:30–17:30 *Invited talk 2: Acquiring Language through Interaction*
Raquel Fernández

17:30–18:00 *Concluding remarks*

Entropy Reduction correlates with temporal lobe activity

Matthew J. Nelson,
Stanislas Dehaene* and **Christophe Pallier**†
Neurospin research center
CEA Saclay
Gif-sur-Yvette 91191 France
{matthew.nelson, stanislas.dehaene, christophe.pallier}@cea.fr

John T. Hale
Linguistics Department
Cornell University
Ithaca, NY 14853 USA
jthale@cornell.edu

Abstract

Using the Entropy Reduction incremental complexity metric, we relate high gamma power signals from the brains of epileptic patients to incremental stages of syntactic analysis in English and French. We find that signals recorded intracranially from the anterior Inferior Temporal Sulcus (aITS) and the posterior Inferior Temporal Gyrus (pITG) correlate with word-by-word Entropy Reduction values derived from phrase structure grammars for those languages. In the anterior region, this correlation persists even in combination with surprisal co-predictors from PCFG and ngram models. The result confirms the idea that the brain's temporal lobe houses a parsing function, one whose incremental processing difficulty profile reflects changes in grammatical uncertainty.

1 Introduction

Incremental complexity metrics connect word-by-word processing data to computational proposals about how parsing might work in the minds of real people. Entropy Reduction is such a metric. It relates the comprehension difficulty that people experience at a word to decreases in uncertainty regarding the grammatical alternatives that are in play at any given point in a sentence (for a review, see Hale 2016). Entropy Reduction plays a key role in accounts of many classic psycholinguistic phenomena (Hale 2003; 2004; 2006) including the difficulty profile of prenominal relative clauses (Yun et al., 2015). It has connected a wide range of behavioral measures to many different theoretical ideas about incremental processing, both with controlled stimuli (Linzen and Jaeger, 2016; Wu et al., 2010) and in naturalistic texts (Frank, 2013). Entropy Reduction and related metrics of grammatical uncertainty have also proved useful in the analysis of EEG data by helping theorists to interpret well-known event-related potentials (beim Graben et al., 2008; beim Graben and Drenhaus, 2012).

This paper applies Entropy Reduction (henceforth: ER) to another type of tightly time-locked brain data: high gamma power electrical signals recorded from the brains of patients awaiting resective surgery for intractable epilepsy. While experimental participants are reading sentences, entropy reductions from phrase structure grammars predict changes in this measured neural signal. This occurred at sites within the temporal lobe that have been implicated, in various ways, in language processing (Fedorenko and Thompson-Schill, 2014; Pallier et al., 2011; Dronkers et al., 2004). The result generalizes across both French and English speakers. The absence of similar correlations in a control condition with word lists suggests that the effect is indeed due to sentence-structural processing. A companion paper explores algorithmic models of this processing (Nelson et al., Under review).

The remainder of this paper is organized into five sections. Section 2 first introduces intracranial recording techniques, as they were applied in our study. Section 3 details the language models that we used, including both hierarchical phrase structure grammars and word-level Markov models. Section 4 goes on to explain the statistical methods, including a complementary "sham" analysis of the word-list control condition where no sentence structure exists. Section 5 reports the results of these analyses (e.g. Table 2 on page 8). Section 6 concludes.

*,†additional affiliation: Université Paris 11
*additional affiliation: Collège de France

Proceedings of the 7th Workshop on Cognitive Modeling and Computational Linguistics (CMCL 2017), pages 1–10,
Valencia, Spain, April 7, ©2017 Association for Computational Linguistics

Site	Number of patients	Language	Recording type
Stanford Medical Center	3	English	ECoG
Massachusetts General Hospital	1	English	Depth
Pitié-Salpêtrière Hospital	8	French	Depth

Table 1: Recording site information.

2 Methods: Intracranial recording

2.1 Overview

In intracranial recording, neurological patients volunteer to perform a task while electrodes, implanted in their brains for clinical reasons, continuously monitor neural activity. It offers the most direct measure possible of neural activity in humans, and as such is attractive to researchers from across many disciplines (Fedorenko et al., 2016; Martin et al., 2016; Rutishauser et al., 2006). Recordings can be made either from the cortical surface (referred to here as ECoG, short for electrocorticogram) or from beneath the cortical surface (referred to here as depth recordings). For both types, what is recorded is a spatial average of extracellular potentials generated by neurons in the vicinity of the recording site. This is the same signal as the EEG signal, which has a millisecond temporal resolution, but with a spatial resolution far improved beyond that of EEG. Despite these benefits, there are also limitations to the technique. The recordings are only made in certain hospitals under quite specialized conditions. The number of subjects recorded from are therefore typically smaller than in studies using non-invasive brain-imaging methods. Also, the signals are obtained from patients with brain pathologies, primarily epilepsy. Nevertheless, the latter concern can be mitigated by screening out participants who perform poorly on clinical tests of language function, by discarding data from regions that are later determined to be pathological, or from trials with epileptic activity (see § 2.3.1).

2.2 Patients

Patients from three different hospitals (Table 1) were recorded while awaiting resective surgery as part of their clinical treatment for intractable epilepsy. Written informed consent was obtained from all participants. Experiments were approved by the corresponding review boards at each institution.

2.3 Recordings

Intracranial voltages were low-pass filtered with a 200 Hz to 300 Hz cutoff and sampled at either 1525.88 Hz (SMC) or 512 Hz (MGH and PS). Electrode positions were localized using the method described in Dykstra et al (2011) and Hermes et al (2010) and converted to standard MNI coordinates. Only left hemisphere electrodes were analyzed.

2.3.1 Channel and artifact removal

In intracranial experiments, a portion of channels often show either flat or extremely noisy recorded signals. In both cases this suggests problems with the recording contact and the channel should in general not be analyzed. As mentioned above, channels recording from tissue that was determined to be pathological should also not be analyzed. Here, raw data for each channel were visually inspected for artifacts, such as large jumps in the data, and for channels with little to no signal variation apparent above the noise levels. 7.9% of channels were removed from further analysis in this manner. 10.5% of channels were clinically determined as showing epileptic activity and were also removed from further analysis.

2.3.2 Referencing

To eliminate potential effects from common-mode noise in the online reference and volume conduction duplicating effects in nearby electrodes, recordings were re-referenced offline using a bipolar montage in which the difference in voltage signals between neighboring electrodes was calculated and used for further analysis. For ECoG grids, such differences were computed for all nearest neighbor pairs along both dimensions of the grid. Electrodes that were identified as noisy or pathological were systematically excluded before pairwise differencing. This procedure resulted in 288 bipolar pairs of ECoG electrodes, and 433 bipolar pairs of depth electrodes available for analysis in this dataset. We took the location of each bipolar pair to be the midpoint between the two individual electrode locations. We hence-

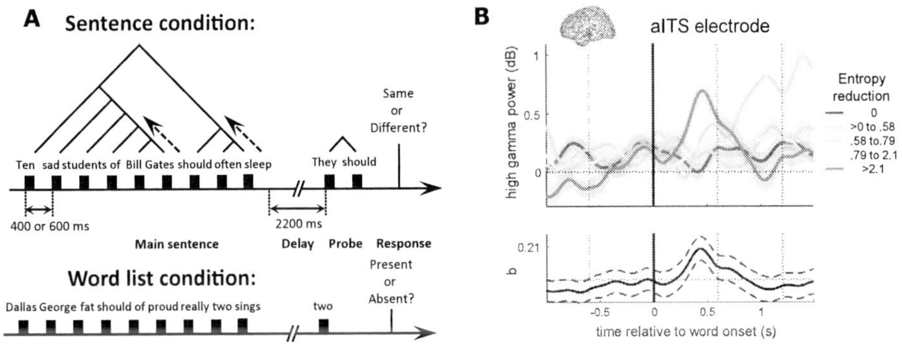

Figure 1: (A) Experimental setup: patients saw sentences or word lists, of variable length, and judged whether a subsequent probe matches or does not match. (B) High-gamma power profile at various levels of Entropy Reduction for the word at time 0. The lower part of panel (B) shows the fitted regression coefficient for Entropy Reduction and its 95% confidence interval across time.

forth refer to these bipolar pairs as electrodes for simplicity. All results presented in this study were essentially unchanged when using an average reference montage.

2.4 Tasks

There were two tasks presented in separate blocks: one in which the stimuli were simple sentences in the participant's native language, and another where the stimuli were randomly-ordered word lists. Figure 1A schematically depicts this arrangement.

In the main sentence task blocks, patients were presented with a sentence of variable length (up to 10 words), followed after a delay of 2.2 seconds by a shorter probe sentence (2-5 words). On 75% of trials, this probe was related to the previous sentence by processes of substitution and ellipsis. For example, a stimulus sentence like "Bill Gates slept in Paris" was followed by probes such as "he did" or "he slept there." On the remaining 25% of trials the probe shared this form, but was unrelated in meaning to the stimulus e.g. "they should." The participants were instructed to press one key if the probe had the SAME meaning and another key if the meaning of the probe was DIFFERENT. This matching task is meant to engage participants' memory for the entire sentence, rather than just one part.

In the word-list task block, patients were presented with the same words used in the preceding sentence task block, but in random order. To avoid any attempt at sentence reconstruction, words were shuffled both within and across sentences. Then following the same delay as in the sentence task, the patients were presented with a one word probe, and asked to identify whether or not that word was in the preceding list. This control task has the same perceptual and motor demands as the main task but with no sequential expectations or sentence-structural interpretation of the stimuli. Sentence and word list tasks were presented in alternating blocks of 80 trials, with 2 to 3 sentence-task blocks and 1 word list block recorded for each patient.

In both sentence and word list conditions, words were presented one at a time at a fixed location on a screen to discourage eye movements. The temporal rate was adapted to individual patients' natural pace, either 400ms (4 patients) or 600ms (8 patients) per word.

3 Materials: language models

We consider two types of language models. The first type comprises linguistically-motivated probabilistic context-free phrase structure grammars (PCFG) based on X-bar theory (Sportiche et al., 2013; Jackendoff, 1977). Figure 2 shows an English example. The hierarchical analyses assigned by this first type of model contrast with those of a second type: word bigram models fitted to Google Ngrams (Michel et al., 2011). Within each type, there are specific English and French versions.

The PCFGs are derived from a computer program that created the stimuli for the intracranial recordings. This program randomly generates well-formed X-bar structures using uniform dis-

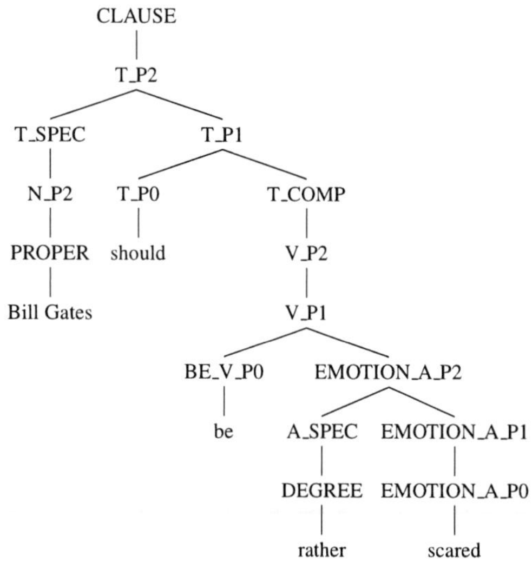

Figure 2: Example analysis from X-bar grammar. $P\{0,1,2\}$ annotations indicate bar level, i.e V_P2 means verb phrase, and *should* is analyzed as a projection of tense (T).

tributions. It decides, for instance, on the number of adjuncts present in a particular phrase, the status of each verb as infinitival, transitive or copular, and on nominal properties such as case, person and number. Applying relative frequency estimation to a sample of these trees, we inferred a PCFG that matches the distributions present in the experimental stimuli. For more on this estimation procedure, see Chi (1999).

These language models serve to predict comprehension difficulty via three different incremental complexity metrics, described below.

3.1 Entropy Reduction

Entropy Reduction (ER) is a complexity metric that tracks uncertainty regarding the proper analysis of sentences. If a word comes in that *decreases* grammatical uncertainty, then the metric predicts effort in proportion to the degree to which uncertainty was reduced. Hale (2016) reviews this metric, its motivation and broader implications. Here we characterize precisely the particular ERs that figure in our modeling by reference to a generic sentence w consisting of two concatenated substrings, u and v. Let $w = uv$ be generated by a PCFG G so that $w \in L(G)$ and denote by D_u the set of derivations that derive the k-word initial substring $u_{0\cdots k}$ as a prefix. This initial substring corresponds to the words that the comprehender has already heard, and may be of any length. The existence of at least one grammatical completion, v, restates the requirement that u be a viable prefix. Since G is a probabilistic grammar, each member $d \in D_u$ has a probability. If the Shannon entropy $H(D_u)$ of this set is reduced in the transition from one initial substring to the next, then information-processing work has been done and neural effort is predicted. We compute the predictions of this metric, in both languages, using the freely-available Cornell Conditional Probability Calculator, or CCPC for short (Chen et al., 2014). This program calculates a probability for each derivation $d \in D_u$, conditioned on the prefix string u. It uses exhaustive chart parsing to compute the total probability of D_u following Nederhof and Satta (2008). In order to focus on sentence-structural aspects of comprehension, we follow previous work such as Demberg and Keller (2008) and Yun et al. (2015) in computing this metric at the pre-terminal, rather than word, level.

3.2 Surprisal

The surprisal of a word, in the sense of Hale (2001), links measurable comprehension difficulty to the (negative log) total probability eliminated in the transition from $u_{0\cdots k}$ to $u_{0\cdots k+1}$. We used the CCPC to compute surprisals at the preterminal level from PCFG models. Surprisals from word-bigram models were obtained simply by negative log-transforming the conditional probability of a successor word given the previous word.

3.3 Bigram entropy

This metric is entropic like ER, but ignores structure and deals only with the conditional probability distribution of the next word. We determined this entropy using the counts of all of the bigrams in the Google N-grams database starting with one of the words in our stimuli. This amounted to over 9.2 million unique bigrams in English and 3.3 million in French. In the analysis to follow, these word-bigram models serve as a comparison to the grammatical predictors rather than any sort of positive proposal about human sentence comprehension.

4 Analysis

4.1 Broadband high gamma power

We analyzed the broadband high-gamma power (HGP), which is broadly accepted in the neurophysiological field as reflecting the average activation and firing rates of the local neuronal population around a recording site (Ray and Maunsell, 2011; Miller et al., 2009). We calculated the HGP using wavelet analyses implemented in the FieldTrip toolbox (Oostenveld et al., 2011). We used a wavelet width of 5 and calculated the spectral power over the frequency window spanning from 70 to 150 Hz sampled in the time domain at 1/4 of the raw sampling rate. The resulting power at each time point was then transformed to a decibel scale relative to the entire experiment mean power for each channel for subsequent analyses. The shading of traces in Figure1B reflects the standard errors of the mean across trials.

4.2 Regression analyses

At the single-electrode level, we performed linear regression analyses with each word as the basic unit of observation. The dependent variable was the HGP, averaged over a window from 200 to 500 ms following each word. It is in this time window, more or less, that linguistic effects have been found in behavioral, EEG and MEG data (Pylkkänen et al., 2014; Bemis and Pylkkänen, 2013; Sahin et al., 2009; Friederici, 2002).

We considered the word-by-word Entropy Reduction (ER), as the covariate of interest. To this, we added two other covariates of no interest. One differentiates closed class and open class words, while another summarizes baseline neural activity. We used for the baseline value the average HGP in a 1-second interval before the onset of the first word of a particular stimulus main sentence. This approach, in which the baseline is included as a covariate, improves over the classical subtraction approach because it only accounts for the variance in the dependent variable in common with the baseline term. However for display purposes, Figure 1B depicts the classical subtraction of signal-minus-baseline.

The models shown in Table 3 include an additional covariate of interest: bigram entropy, bigram surprisal and phrase structure surprisal, as introduced above in section 3. The four regression models were thus:

$$\text{HGP} \sim 1 + \text{ER} + \text{Word Class} + \text{Baseline} \qquad \text{(I)}$$

$$\begin{aligned}\text{HGP} \sim 1 + \text{ER} &+ \text{bigram entropy} \\ &+ \text{Word Class} + \text{Baseline}\end{aligned} \qquad \text{(II)}$$

$$\begin{aligned}\text{HGP} \sim 1 + \text{ER} &+ \text{bigram surprisal} \\ &+ \text{Word Class} + \text{Baseline}\end{aligned} \qquad \text{(III)}$$

$$\begin{aligned}\text{HGP} \sim 1 + \text{ER} &+ \text{PCFG surprisal} \\ &+ \text{Word Class} + \text{Baseline}\end{aligned} \qquad \text{(IV)}$$

We observed the same patterns of results described in this paper when including all of the parameters in one larger model.

4.3 Word list sham analyses

If uncertainty about grammatical structures is indeed driving ER effects when the stimulus is a sentence, then these effects should be stronger than corresponding effects for the same words presented in a random, non-sentential order. To test this, we assigned sham ER values to the word list condition that matched the value in the sentence condition in one of two ways. In Method 1 (word identity matching), each word in the word-list condition was matched to the same word when it occurred in the list condition (possibly at a different position). In Method 2 (word ordinal position matching), each trial in the word-list condition was matched to a trial of the same length in the sentence-task condition. The ER values of the sentence-task trial were then assigned to the word-list trial, matched by ordinal position. We then compared the effect of the real ER values in the sentence task versus the sham values assigned to the word-list task by computing the interaction of that variable across tasks for each sham assignment method. These analyses control for the possibility that either ordinal word position or individual word identity underlie the effects observed in the sentence-task condition.

4.4 Statistical tests

Mixed-effects regression models have become standard in computational psycholinguistics. However sample sizes in intracranial studies are not usually as large, for the reasons mentioned above in subsection 2.1. In such a scenario multilevel models typically gain little beyond classical varying-coefficient models (Gelman and Hill, 2007). We therefore pursued a statistical approach that independently assesses statistical significance across electrodes and participants using two different testing procedures. To make inferences about particular brain areas rather than analyzing the entire heterogeneous sample at once, we pursued this approach in a regions of interest (ROIs) based analysis. Both procedures use as inputs the z-scores of coefficients from the above multiple regression analysis for each electrode located within a given ROI. We derived the z-scores from the p-values of the t-statistics of the coefficients, which account for the degrees of freedom of each test.

The first test tests for significance across electrodes ignoring participant identification using Stouffers z-score method (Zaykin, 2011). This method tests the significance of the z-score sum across electrodes with an assumption of independence between electrodes. Though its independence assumption is likely violated in these data, the test provides a useful benchmark. This test is complemented by the second test that does not make this assumption.

The second test tests for significance across participants (i.e. treating participants as a random factor) using a randomization/simulation procedure that proceeded as follows. For each participant, we observed the highest (and lowest) z-score for all electrodes in the ROI, and calculated the average of these scores across participants that had any electrodes in the ROI. We then simulated independent random z-scores sampled from a standard normal distribution for every electrode in the ROI, with each simulated electrode assigned to a subject to give the same distribution of the number of electrodes per each subject in the ROI found in the real data. With each iteration of the simulation we calculated the mean of the highest simulated z-scores across subjects in the same manner as with the real data, repeating this 100,000 times to obtain a simulated null-distribution of the across-subject mean best z-score expected by chance. The mean highest (and absolute value of the lowest) z-scores across subjects in the actual data were then compared to this null distribution to ascertain the probability of recording such a value of equal or greater extremity in the sample by chance.

By testing whether the effect is consistently observed across multiple participants, this second test avoids concerns about dependence between electrodes. This test benefits from the sensitivity afforded by testing for the best electrode in each subject, especially appropriate in an intracranial recording scenario with a relatively small number of electrodes that are not necessarily positioned at the ideal location for a given effect in each subject. The first test complements this by showing significance over the entire pool of electrodes, not relying on subjects' best electrodes.

Note that an alternate approach for the first test would be to count the number of electrodes in each region with a positive effect significant at the 0.05 level, and use a binomial test to assess the probability of observing at least that many significant electrodes by chance given the total number of electrodes in that region. We prefer Stouffer's z-score method because it does not rely on an arbitrary 0.05 threshold to determine the overall p-value, and because it takes into account the total contribution of every z-score in the sample. We thus chose to report the Stouffers z-score test results only, though we note that the proportions of significant electrodes here support the same patterns of significance.

4.5 Regions of interest (ROI) definition

We defined ROIs independently of our theoretical predictors by finding local maxima of the difference between sentences and baseline activity. The procedure to find these locations proceeded as follows: For each electrode a z-score of the contrast between activation during the sentence and during the baseline period was calculated. A potential ROI center was systematically placed at all possible locations in a 3D grid in the cortex, with 1 mm between possible locations in all directions. The ROI radius was fixed to 22 mm. At each position, the electrodes within the fixed distance from the ROI center were grouped to calculate two independent z-scores. These z-scores were calculated using much the same procedure as above, except that a t-test across the means of subjects was used to assess the across-subjects' z-score, rather than simulations. This avoidance of numerical simulation saved computing time. The two z-scores were combined via a weighted average to determine a composite z-score for each ROI, with a weight of 0.25 and 0.75 assigned to the across-electrodes and across-subjects z-scores respectively. Local maxima of the composite z-score were then detected and ordered according to the composite z-score, discarding local maxima within 22 mm of an-

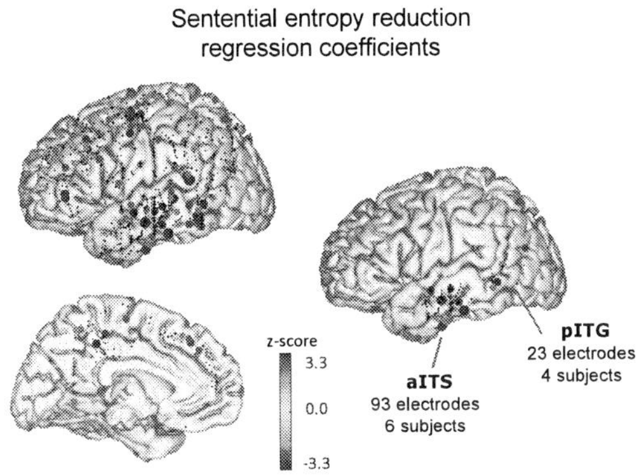

Figure 3: Entropy reduction regression coefficients. Each dot represents an electrode (aggregated across subjects), with size and color saturation reflecting the corresponding z-score for the coefficient corresponding to ER. Z-scores below an absolute value threshold of 1.96 are plotted with a black dot. Electrodes located >10mm from midline are projected onto the lateral surface plot (top), others are projected onto the midline plot (bottom). (Right) The electrodes included in the aITS and pITG ROIs are shown.

other local maxima with a higher z-score. The two highest-scoring local maxima with an anterior/posterior MNI coordinate more posterior than -8 were selected as the ROI centers. These had MNI coordinates: -37,-16,-27 (aITS) and -47,-66,1 (pITG). Figure 3 shows the locations of electrodes within each of these regions.

5 Results & Discussion

ER was observed to correlate with an increase in activity as suggested in Figure 1B on page 3, where data from just one electrode are plotted. Figure 3, above, shows the distribution of the effect across the entire sample. Groups of positive coefficients were observed in the aITS and pITG ROIs, which, as Table 2 shows, were significant across subjects and electrodes. A comparison with sham ER values assigned to the word list task showed that the effect in both areas was significantly higher than word identity matched sham values in the word list task (Table 2, middle). The coefficients in aITS but not pITG were significantly higher than ordinal position matched sham values in the word list task (Table 2, bottom).

In additional multiple regression models, we included other entropy- and surprisal- based predictors alongside ER in two-parameter models. Table 3 shows that there was a significant negative effect of bigram entropy and a positive effect of bigram surprisal in both aITS and pITG, with no effect of PCFG surprisal in either region. ER is still significant in combination with each of these covariates, except with bigram surprisal in pITG, which was significant across subjects but not across electrodes. Overall, we find that ER is positively correlated with temporal activity after accounting for lexical effects and surprisal in its conventional version.

6 Conclusion

Intracranial recordings from patients reading sentences show a correlation with ER in anterior Inferior Temporal Sulcus (aITS) and posterior Inferior Temporal Gyrus (pITG). This occurred even when potential contributions to neural activity from word identity or ordinal position in sentences were accounted for in a control task where there was no syntactic structure. Additionally, aITS and pITG showed a negative response to bigram entropy and a positive response to bigram surprisal. However, the ER effect persisted in aITS when combined with these and other potentially competing effects. These results converge with other findings based on reading time (Wu et al., 2010; Linzen and Jaeger, 2016) that suggest that downward changes in grammatical uncertainty can serve as an approximate quantitative index of human processing effort. We did also observe a positive effect of lexical bigram surprisal, especially in pITG, which has been observed in other work (Nelson et al., Under review), though we focus here on ER.

These results add a precise anatomical localization to this earlier body of work, converging well with findings from MEG (Brennan and Pylkkänen, 2016; van Schijndel et al., 2015), PET (Mazoyer et al., 1993; Stowe et al., 1998) and fMRI (Brennan et al., 2012). As with any correlational modeling result, there is no suggestion of exhaustivity. We do not claim that X-bar grammars are the only ones whose Entropy Reductions would model HGP. But they suffice to do so. This lends credence to the idea, recently underlined by van Schijndel and Schuler (2015), that phrase structure of some sort must figure in realistic models of word-by-word human sentence comprehension.

	Sentences					
	Stouffer's Z		Mean highest Z-score		Mean lowest Z-score	
region	value	p	value	p	value	p
ant. Inferior Temporal Sulcus	**6.01**	**< 0.001**	**3.53**	**< 0.001**	-0.99	0.997
post. Inferior Temporal Gyrus	**4.69**	**< 0.001**	**2.42**	**< 0.001**	-0.87	0.862
	Sentences vs. Word lists- word identity match					
ant. Inferior Temporal Sulcus	**4.23**	**< 0.001**	**2.18**	**0.013**	-1.53	0.642
post. Inferior Temporal Gyrus	**3.42**	**< 0.001**	1.77	0.050	-0.87	0.862
	Sentences vs. Word lists- word ordinal position match					
ant. Inferior Temporal Sulcus	**2.80**	**0.005**	**2.21**	**0.009**	-1.61	0.497
post. Inferior Temporal Gyrus	1.95	0.051	1.49	0.204	-1.22	0.491

Table 2: Hypothesis tests for fitted regression coefficients on model I for Entropy Reduction predictor by region of interest (ROI). The first two columns report statistics obtained using Stouffer's Z-score method, pooling electrodes across human participants. Subsequent columns report the highest and lowest z-score values on a per-participant basis, averaged across participants. The p-values for the mean highest and lowest z-scores were determined using simulations, see § 4.4. The middle and lower tables show the interaction of the regressor across the sentence and word list tasks after assigning sham values to the word list that were matched with the sentence condition values of the same word identity (Middle) and word ordinal position (Bottom). Positive values in these cases indicates a more positive coefficient in the sentence task.

		aITS					
		Stouffer's Z		Mean highest Z-score		Mean lowest Z-score	
	predictor	value	p	value	p	value	p
(II)	Entropy reduction	**5.43**	**< 0.001**	**3.22**	**< 0.001**	-1.05	0.994
(II)	Bigram entropy	**-2.53**	**0.011**	1.32	0.881	**-2.34**	**0.002**
(III)	Entropy reduction	**4.70**	**< 0.001**	**2.58**	**< 0.001**	-1.08	0.991
(III)	Bigram surprisal	**2.31**	**0.021**	**2.53**	**< 0.001**	-1.27	0.932
(IV)	Entropy reduction	**6.05**	**< 0.001**	**3.38**	**< 0.001**	-0.91	0.999
	Phrase structure surprisal	-1.16	0.246	1.24	0.951	-1.46	0.741

		pITG					
		Stouffer's Z		Mean highest Z-score		Mean lowest Z-score	
	predictor	value	p	value	p	value	p
(II)	Entropy reduction	**4.11**	**< 0.001**	**2.38**	**< 0.001**	-0.97	0.779
(II)	Bigram entropy	**-2.33**	**0.02**	1.54	0.166	**-2.26**	**0.002**
(III)	Entropy reduction	1.63	0.104	**1.98**	**0.013**	-1.61	0.119
(III)	Bigram surprisal	**7.56**	**< 0.001**	**5.61**	**< 0.001**	-0.29	0.999
(IV)	Entropy reduction	**4.87**	**< 0.001**	**2.22**	**0.002**	-0.5	0.990
	Phrase structure surprisal	-1.29	0.196	0.97	0.777	-1.7	0.078

Table 3: Hypothesis tests for fitted regression coefficients for two parameter models including a different co-factor of interest with the Entropy Reduction regressor. Each pair of rows corresponds to the two coefficients of a different two parameter model. Results are shown in the same format as Table 2.

Acknowledgments

This research was supported by an ERC grant "NeuroSyntax" to S.D., the Agence Nationale de la Recherche (ANR, France, Contract # 140301), the Fondation Roger de Spoelberch, and the Fondation Bettencourt Schueller. We thank Peter beim Graben for helpful comments on the manuscript. We would also like to thank Josef Parvizi, Lionel Naccache and Sydney Cash for their collaboration. We thank Profs. Michel Baulac and Vincent Navarro, and Drs. Claude Adam, Katia Lehongre and Stephane Clémenceau for their help with SEEG recordings in Paris. For assistance in data collection we acknowledge Imen el Karoui, Kristof Giber, Vinitha Rangarajan, Sandra Gattas, Xiaofang Yang, the medical staff at Stanford Medical Center, Massachusetts General Hospital and the Pitié-Salpêtrière Hospital, as well as our 12 patients for their participation. We thank Laurent Cohen for input during the project's conception, and Hilda Koopman for assistance in designing the stimuli.

References

Douglas K. Bemis and Liina Pylkkänen. 2013. Flexible Composition: MEG Evidence for the Deployment of Basic Combinatorial Linguistic Mechanisms in Response to Task Demands. *PLoS ONE*, 8(9), September.

Jonathan R. Brennan and Liina Pylkkänen. 2016. Meg evidence for incremental sentence composition in the anterior temporal lobe. *Cognitive Science*, page Online Version of Record published before inclusion in an issue.

Jonathan Brennan, Yuval Nir, Uri Hasson, Rafael Malach, David J. Heeger, and Liina Pylkkänen. 2012. Syntactic structure building in the anterior temporal lobe during natural story listening. *Brain and Language*, 120(2):163 – 173.

Zhong Chen, Jiwon Yun, Tim Hunter, and John Hale. 2014. Modeling sentence processing difficulty with a conditional probability calculator. In *Proceedings of the* 36th *Annual Cognitive Science Conference*, pages 1856–1857.

Zhiyi Chi. 1999. Statistical properties of probabilistic context-free grammars. *Computational Linguistics, Volume25, number l, March 1999*, 25(1):131–160.

Vera Demberg and Frank Keller. 2008. Data from eye-tracking corpora as evidence for theories of syntactic processing complexity. *Cognition*, 109(2):193–210.

Nina F. Dronkers, David P. Wilkins, Robert D. Van Valin, Brenda B. Redfern, and Jeri J. Jaeger. 2004. Lesion analysis of the brain areas involved in language comprehension: Towards a new functional anatomy of language. *Cognition*, 92(1-2):145–177.

Andrew R. Dykstra, Alexander M. Chan, Brian T. Quinn, Rodrigo Zepeda, Corey J. Keller, Justine Cormier, Joseph R. Madsen, Emad N. Eskandar, and Sydney S. Cash. 2011. Individualized localization and cortical surface-based registration of intracranial electrodes. *NeuroImage*.

Evelina Fedorenko and Sharon L. Thompson-Schill. 2014. Reworking the language network. *Trends in cognitive sciences*, 18(3):120–126.

Evelina Fedorenko, Terri L. Scott, Peter Brunner, William G. Coon, Brianna Pritchett, Gerwin Schalk, and Nancy Kanwisher. 2016. Neural correlate of the construction of sentence meaning. *Proceedings of the National Academy of Sciences*, 113(41):E6256–E6262.

Stefan L. Frank. 2013. Uncertainty reduction as a measure of cognitive load in sentence comprehension. *Topics in Cognitive Science*, 5(3):475–494.

Angela D. Friederici. 2002. Towards a neural basis of auditory sentence processing. *Trends in Cognitive Sciences*, 6(2):78–84, February.

Andrew Gelman and Jennifer Hill. 2007. *Data Analysis Using Regression and Multilevel/Hierarchical Models*. Cambridge University Press. Google-Books-ID: c9xLKzZWoZ4C.

Peter beim Graben and Heiner Drenhaus. 2012. Computationelle neurolinguistik. *Zeitschrift für germanistische Linguistik*, 40(1):97–125. In German.

Peter beim Graben, Sabrina Gerth, and Shravan Vasishth. 2008. Towards dynamical system models of language-related brain potentials. *Cognitive Neurodynamics*, 2(3):229 – 255.

John Hale. 2001. A probabilistic Earley parser as a psycholinguistic model. In *Proceedings of the Second Meeting of the North American Chapter of the Association for Computational Linguistics*.

John Hale. 2003. The information conveyed by words in sentences. *Journal of Psycholinguistic Research*, 32(2):101–123, March.

John Hale. 2004. The information-processing difficulty of incremental parsing. In Frank Keller, Stephen Clark, Matthew Crocker, and Mark Steedman, editors, *Proceedings of the ACL Workshop on Incremental Parsing: bringing engineering and cognition together*, pages 58–65.

John Hale. 2006. Uncertainty about the rest of the sentence. *Cognitive Science*, 30(4):609–642.

John Hale. 2016. Information-theoretical complexity metrics. *Language and Linguistics Compass*, pages 1–16.

Dora Hermes, Kai J. Miller, Herke Jan Noordmans, Mariska J. Vansteensel, and Nick F. Ramsey. 2010. Automated electrocorticographic electrode localization on individually rendered brain surfaces. *Journal of neuroscience methods*, 185(2):293–298.

Ray Jackendoff. 1977. *$\bar{X}$ Syntax: A Study of Phrase Structure*. MIT Press, Cambridge, Mass.

Tal Linzen and T. Florian Jaeger. 2016. Uncertainty and expectation in sentence processing: Evidence from subcategorization distributions. *Cognitive Science*, 40(6):1382–1411.

Stephanie Martin, José del R. Millán, Robert T. Knight, and Brian N. Pasley. 2016. The use of intracranial recordings to decode human language: Challenges and opportunities. *Brain and Language*, page Corrected Proof Available online 1 July 2016.

Bernard M. Mazoyer, Nathalie Tzourio, Victor Frak, Andre Syrota, Nina Murayama, Olivier Levrier, Georges Salamon, Stanislas Dehaene, Laurent Cohen, and Jacques Mehler. 1993. The cortical representation of speech. *Journal of Cognitive Neuroscience*, 5(4):467–479.

Jean-Baptiste Michel, Yuan Kui Shen, Aviva Presser Aiden, Adrian Veres, Matthew K. Gray, The Google Books Team, Joseph P. Pickett, Dale Hoiberg, Dan Clancy, Peter Norvig, Jon Orwant, Steven Pinker, Martin A. Nowak, and Erez Lieberman Aiden. 2011. Quantitative Analysis of Culture Using Millions of Digitized Books. *Science*, 331(6014):176–182, January.

Kai J. Miller, Larry B. Sorensen, Jeffrey G. Ojemann, and Marcel Den Nijs. 2009. Power-law scaling in the brain surface electric potential. *PLoS computational biology*, 5(12).

Mark-Jan Nederhof and Giorgio Satta. 2008. Computing partition functions of PCFGs. *Research on Language and Computation*, 6(2):139–162.

Matthew J. Nelson, Imen El Karoui, Kristof Giber, Xiaofang Yang, Laurent Cohen, Hilda Koopman, Lionel Naccache, John T. Hale, Christophe Pallier, and Stanislas Dehaene. Under review. Neurophysiological dynamics of phrase structure building during sentence processing.

Robert Oostenveld, Pascal Fries, Eric Maris, and Jan-Mathijs Schoffelen. 2011. FieldTrip: open source software for advanced analysis of MEG, EEG, and invasive electrophysiological data. *Computational intelligence and neuroscience*, 2011.

Christophe Pallier, Anne-Dominique Devauchelle, and Stanislas Dehaene. 2011. Cortical representation of the constituent structure of sentences. *Proceedings of the National Academy of Sciences*, 108(6):2522–2527, 02.

Liina Pylkkänen, Douglas K. Bemis, and Estibaliz Blanco Elorrieta. 2014. Building phrases in language production: An MEG study of simple composition. *Cognition*, 133(2):371–384, November.

Supratim Ray and John H. R. Maunsell. 2011. Different Origins of Gamma Rhythm and High-Gamma Activity in Macaque Visual Cortex. *PLOS Biol*, 9(4):e1000610.

Ueli Rutishauser, Adam N. Mamelak, and Erin M. Schuman. 2006. Single-trial learning of novel stimuli by individual neurons of the human hippocampus-amygdala complex. *Neuron*, 49(6):805–813.

Ned T. Sahin, Steven Pinker, Sydney S. Cash, Donald Schomer, and Eric Halgren. 2009. Sequential Processing of Lexical, Grammatical, and Phonological Information Within Broca's Area. *Science*, 326(5951):445–449, October.

Dominique Sportiche, Hilda Koopman, and Edward Stabler. 2013. *An Introduction to Syntactic Analysis and Theory*. Wiley-Blackwell.

Laurie A. Stowe, Cees A. J. Broere, Anne M. J. Paans, Albertus A. Wijers, Gijsbertus Mulder, Wim Vaalburg, and Frans Zwarts. 1998. Localizing components of a complex task: Sentence processing and working memory. *Neuroreport*, 9(13):2995–2999.

Marten van Schijndel and William Schuler. 2015. Hierarchic syntax improves reading time prediction. In *Proceedings of NAACL 2015*, Denver, Colorado, USA, June. Association for Computational Linguistics.

Marten van Schijndel, Brian Murphy, and William Schuler. 2015. Evidence of syntactic working memory usage in MEG data. In *Proceedings of CMCL 2015*, Denver, Colorado, USA, June. Association for Computational Linguistics.

Stephen Wu, Asaf Bachrach, Carlos Cardenas, and William Schuler. 2010. Complexity metrics in an incremental right-corner parser. In *Proceedings of the 48th Annual Meeting of the Association for Computational Linguistics*, pages 1189–1198, Uppsala, Sweden, July. Association for Computational Linguistics.

Jiwon Yun, Zhong Chen, Tim Hunter, John Whitman, and John Hale. 2015. Uncertainty in processing relative clauses across East Asian languages. *Journal of East Asian Linguistics*, 24(2):113–148.

Dmitri V. Zaykin. 2011. Optimally weighted Z-test is a powerful method for combining probabilities in meta-analysis. *Journal of evolutionary biology*, 24(8):1836–1841, August.

Learning an Input Filter for Argument Structure Acquisition

Laurel Perkins
Dept. of Linguistics
University of Maryland
College Park, MD 20742
perkinsl@umd.edu

Naomi H. Feldman
Dept. of Linguistics & UMIACS
University of Maryland
College Park, MD 20742
nhf@umd.edu

Jeffrey Lidz
Dept. of Linguistics
University of Maryland
College Park, MD 20742
jlidz@umd.edu

Abstract

How do children learn a verb's argument structure when their input contains non-basic clauses that obscure verb transitivity? Here we present a new model that infers verb transitivity by learning to filter out non-basic clauses that were likely parsed in error. In simulations with child-directed speech, we show that this model accurately categorizes the majority of 50 frequent transitive, intransitive and alternating verbs, and jointly learns appropriate parameters for filtering parsing errors. Our model is thus able to filter out problematic data for verb learning without knowing in advance which data need to be filtered.

1 Introduction

Young language learners are limited by partial knowledge in identifying the structure of sentences they hear and of their language in general. This partial knowledge may lead to inaccurate parses of their input, resulting in data that are misleading about the true structure of their language. Here we investigate a problem of misleading data in verb learning: how learners identify verbs' syntactic properties despite the presence of unknown grammatical structures that obscure those properties.

We propose a new model for the acquisition of argument structure, the syntactic property of a verb that determines which types of clauses it can occur in (Chomsky, 1965; Chomsky, 1981; Grimshaw, 1990). We model how a learner can use verb distributions to infer whether a verb can occur in a transitive clause with both a subject and an object, an intransitive clause with only a subject, or both. This inference depends on the ability to accurately perceive the arguments in a clause: whether a clause has a subject and an object, or only a subject. Identifying these arguments is straightforward for "basic" clause types like (1) and (2), but more difficult for "non-basic" clause types that do not follow the subject-verb-object word order typical of English, like (3):

(1) John ate a sandwich. Amy threw a frisbee.

(2) John ate. (*Amy threw.)

(3) What did John eat? What did Amy throw?

A learner tracking when direct objects are present after the verb would notice that sentences like (1) contain both subjects and objects, and sentences like (2) contain only subjects. It would then follow that *throw* is obligatorily transitive whereas *eat* can alternate. But this strategy is complicated by the wh-object questions in (3). These questions do not have direct objects after the verb, but do have two arguments: the wh-word *what* stands in for the verb's object. These data may be misleading for a child who has not yet learned how to identify wh-questions in her language. She might note the absence of a direct object after the verb and perceive the sentences in (3) as intransitive, mistakenly concluding that *throw* can alternate just like *eat*.

To learn verb transitivity, learners need some way to filter out the non-basic clauses in their input; this ability is assumed in prominent theories of verb learning such as syntactic and semantic bootstrapping (Gleitman, 1990; Lidz and Gleitman, 2004; Pinker, 1984; Pinker, 1989). In this paper we present a Bayesian model that learns the parameters for such a filter solely by tracking the distributions of verbs with and without direct objects. The model does so under the assumption that some sentence observations will be generated in error, due to mis-parses of non-basic clauses like (3). In simulations with child-directed speech, we show that this model can learn the parameters for

Proceedings of the 7th Workshop on Cognitive Modeling and Computational Linguistics (CMCL 2017), pages 11–19,
Valencia, Spain, April 7, ©2017 Association for Computational Linguistics

filtering these parsing errors in order to categorize 50 verbs as transitive, intransitive, or alternating. We thus demonstrate that it is possible for a learner to learn an input filter for verb learning without knowing in advance what needs to be filtered.

2 Filtering Input

Many have proposed that learners need some way to filter the data they use in acquiring their language (Adriaans and Swingley, 2012; Lidz and Gleitman, 2004; Pearl and Lidz, 2009; Pinker, 1984). This filtering is important for theories of verb learning under which children rely on systematic relations between verbs' syntactic properties and their meanings, e.g. semantic and syntactic bootstrapping (Fisher et al., 2010; Gleitman, 1990; Landau and Gleitman, 1985; Lasnik, 1989; Pinker, 1984; Pinker, 1989). Non-basic clauses obscure these relations, so learners need a way to filter them out of the data they use for verb learning.

Pinker (1984) posits two solutions: either parents might do the filtering and avoid producing these sentences in their children's presence, or children might internally filter these sentences themselves. Parental filtering does not seem to occur: even before their second birthday, English-learning children hear a large number of wh-questions (between 10-17% of their total input), the majority of which do not follow the typical word order of English (Stromswold, 1995). These non-basic clause types are thus prevalent in child-directed speech, necessitating a different filtering solution.

The second logical solution is internal filtering: perhaps children can filter out non-basic clauses themselves. This proposal implicitly assumes that children know which sentences to filter out. However, experimental evidence suggests that children may not have the ability to recognize which sentences contain wh-questions before the age of 20 months, an age at which substantial verb learning is already taking place (Gagliardi et al., 2016). Furthermore, this ability may depend on prior verb knowledge. Identifying that sentences like (3) contain object wh-questions requires the learner to detect when a fronted phrase (like *what*, *who*, or *which NP*) stands in relation to a verb that needs a patient argument and is locally missing one. But this requires the learner to know which verbs take patient arguments, in order to notice when those arguments are needed and missing. In other words, the learner needs to detect that these sentences contain direct object gaps, rather than intransitive uses of these verbs— but in order to do so, the learner must know which verbs are transitive.

The filtering problem thus risks being circular: learners need to know which verbs are transitive in order to detect the signals of non-basic clause types like object wh-questions, but they also need to filter out sentences containing these clause types in order to learn which verbs are transitive. Pinker (1984) posits that children might avoid this problem by using sentence meaning, context, and intonation to identify a filter on their input. Our approach, by contrast, does not require learners to know the parameters of the input filter before they are able to learn verbs. Instead of fixing one of these pieces of knowledge to learn the other, children may jointly infer which verbs are transitive and the parameters for filtering sentences containing non-basic clauses. We thus model a learner who can filter out errors in parsing non-basic clauses, without needing to first identify where those errors came from.

3 Model

Our model uses the distribution of direct objects within and across verbs to infer both verb transitivity and the parameters for filtering non-basic clauses. We adopt a Bayesian framework, in which a learner observes a data pattern and infers the probability of some properties of the system that may have generated that data. This framework conveniently allows us to specify the alternative systems (verb transitivity properties vs. mis-parses of non-basic clauses) that our learner considers for the verb distributions it observes. Our model follows other Bayesian approaches to argument structure acquisition (Alishahi and Stevenson, 2008; Perfors et al., 2010), but considers a different problem than the one explored in that literature. Instead of learning which verb classes exist in a particular language, our model is designed to solve the problem of learning which verbs map to which known transitivity classes despite input that obscures these mappings.

3.1 Generative Model

The model learns from observations of direct objects or no direct objects in sentences containing particular verbs. These observations are formalized as the Bernoulli random variable X in the graphical model in Figure 1. Each $X^{(v)}$ represents an observation from a sentence containing verb v in the model's input, with a value of 1 if the sentence

Figure 1: Graphical Model

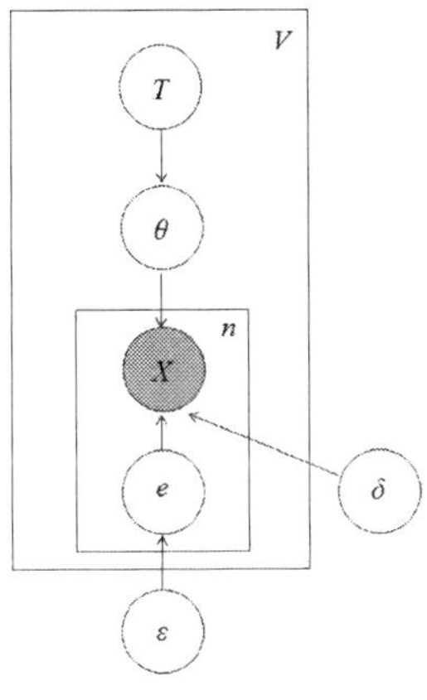

contains a direct object and 0 if it does not. These observations can be generated by two processes: the transitivity of verb v, represented by the variables T and θ in the upper half of the model, or an internal parsing error, represented by the variables e, ϵ, and δ in the lower half of the model. We will describe each of these processes in turn.

In the upper half of the model, each $X^{(v)}$ is conditioned on the parameter $\theta^{(v)}$, a continuous random variable defined for values from 0 to 1 inclusive. This parameter controls how frequently a verb v will be used with a direct object: the learner assumes that for every observation $X^{(v)}$, a biased coin is flipped to determine whether the sentence contains a direct object, with probability $\theta^{(v)}$, or does not, with probability $1 - \theta^{(v)}$.

The parameter $\theta^{(v)}$ is conditioned on the variable $T^{(v)}$, which represents the transitivity of verb v. T is a discrete random variable that can take on three values, corresponding to transitive, intransitive, and alternating verbs. Each of these values determines a different distribution over θ. For the transitive category of T, θ always equals 1: the verb should always occur with a direct object. For the intransitive category, θ always equals 0: the verb should never occur with a direct object. For the alternating category, θ takes a value between 0 and 1 inclusive. The prior probability distribution over θ in this case is a uniform $Beta(1,1)$ distribution.

In the lower half of the model, each X is conditioned on a Bernoulli random variable e, which represents the input filter. If $e_i^{(v)} = 0$, the observation in $X_i^{(v)}$ was generated by $\theta^{(v)}$ and $T^{(v)}$, and accurately reflects the transitivity of verb v. But if $e_i^{(v)} = 1$, the observation in $X_i^{(v)}$ was generated by an internal parsing error, meaning the learner did not have adequate grammatical knowledge to parse the sentence correctly. This observation was not generated by $\theta^{(v)}$ and $T^{(v)}$, and may not accurately reflect the transitivity of verb v, so it should be ignored for the purpose of inferring $T^{(v)}$. Each $e^{(v)}$ is conditioned on the variable ϵ, which represents the probability of an internal parsing error occurring for any verb in the input. The model learns a single parameter value for ϵ across all verbs.

The second parameter of the input filter is δ, which represents the probability of observing a direct object when an observation was generated by an internal parsing error. Thus, whether a sentence contains a direct object or no direct object depends on one of two biased coins. If $e_i^{(v)} = 0$ and the observation accurately reflects the verb's transitivity properties, then one biased coin is flipped and the sentence contains a direct object with probability $\theta^{(v)}$. If $e_i^{(v)} = 0$ and the observation was generated by a parsing error, then a different biased coin is flipped and the sentence contains a direct object with probability δ. Like ϵ, δ is a shared parameter across all verbs. We assume that both ϵ and δ have a uniform $Beta(1,1)$ prior distribution.

3.2 Joint Inference

We use Gibbs sampling (Geman and Geman, 1984) to jointly infer T, ϵ, and δ, integrating over θ and summing over e, with Metropolis-Hastings (Hastings, 1970) proposals for ϵ and δ.

We begin by randomly initializing ϵ and δ, and sampling values of T for each verb given values for those input filter parameters. From observations of a verb with and without direct objects, the model determines which value of T was most likely to have generated those observations. For $k^{(v)}$ direct objects in $n^{(v)}$ sentences containing verb v, we use Bayes' rule to compute the posterior probability of each value for $T^{(v)}$,

$$P(T^{(v)}|k^{(v)}, \epsilon, \delta) = \frac{P(k^{(v)}|T^{(v)}, \epsilon, \delta)P(T^{(v)})}{\sum_{T^{(v)}} P(k^{(v)}|T^{(v)}, \epsilon, \delta)P(T^{(v)})} \quad (4)$$

Bayes' Rule tells us that the posterior probability of a particular value of T given $k^{(v)}$ and the other model parameters is proportional to the likelihood, the probability of $k^{(v)}$ given that value of T and those parameters, and the prior, the probability of

T before seeing any data. We assume that T is independent of ϵ and δ, and that all three values of T have equal prior probability.

To calculate the likelihood, we must sum over e. This sum is intractable, but because all of the values of e for the same verb and the same direct object status are exchangeable, we make the computation more tractable by simply considering how *many* errors were generated for sentences with and without direct objects for a particular verb. We divide the $k^{(v)}$ observed direct objects for a verb into $k_1^{(v)}$ direct objects that were observed accurately and $k_0^{(v)}$ direct objects that were observed in error. The total $n^{(v)}$ observations for verb v are likewise divided into $n_1^{(v)}$ accurate observations and $n_0^{(v)}$ errorful observations. We then calculate the likelihood by marginalizing over $n_1^{(v)}$ and $k_1^{(v)}$, again assuming independence among T, ϵ, and δ,

$$p(k^{(v)}|T^{(v)}, \epsilon, \delta) = \sum_{n_1^{(v)}=0}^{n^{(v)}} \left[\sum_{k_1^{(v)}=0}^{k^{(v)}} p(k^{(v)}|k_1^{(v)}, n_1^{(v)}, \delta) \; p(k_1^{(v)}|n_1^{(v)}, T^{(v)}) \right] p(n_1^{(v)}|\epsilon) \quad (5)$$

The first term in the inner sum is equivalent to $p(k_0^{(v)}|n_0^{(v)}, \delta)$, assuming we know $n^{(v)}$, the total number of observations for a particular verb. This is the probability of observing $k_0^{(v)}$ errorful direct objects out of $n_0^{(v)}$ errorful observations, which follows a binomial distribution with parameter δ. The second term in the inner sum is the probability of observing $k_1^{(v)}$ accurate direct objects out of $n_1^{(v)}$ accurate observations, which follows a binomial distribution with parameter $\theta^{(v)}$. Recall that $\theta^{(v)} = 1$ for the transitive category of T, and $\theta^{(v)} = 0$ for the intransitive category of T. For the alternating verb category, $\theta^{(v)}$ is unknown, so we integrate over all possible values of $\theta^{(v)}$ to obtain $\frac{1}{n_1^{(v)}+1}$. The last term in (5) is the probability of observing $n_1^{(v)}$ accurate observations out of the total $n^{(v)}$ observations for verb v, which follows a binomial distribution with parameter $1 - \epsilon$.

After sampling values for T for each verb in the dataset, we then sample values for ϵ and δ. If T denotes the set of values $T^{(1)}, T^{(2)}, ..., T^{(V)}$, and k denotes the full set of observations of direct objects $k^{(1)}, k^{(2)}, ..., k^{(V)}$ for all V verbs in the input, we can define functions proportional to the posterior distributions on ϵ and δ, $f(\epsilon) \propto p(\epsilon|T, k, \delta)$ and $g(\delta) \propto p(\delta|T, k, \epsilon)$, as

$$f(\epsilon) = p(k|T, \epsilon, \delta)p(\epsilon) \quad (6)$$

$$g(\delta) = p(k|T, \epsilon, \delta)p(\delta) \quad (7)$$

where the likelihood $p(k|T, \epsilon, \delta)$ is the product over all verbs v of $p(k^{(v)}|T^{(v)}, \epsilon, \delta)$, as calculated in (5).

Within the Gibbs sampler, we resample ϵ using 10 iterations of a Metropolis-Hastings algorithm. We begin by randomly initializing ϵ. At each iteration, we propose a new value ϵ', sampled from the proposal distribution $Q(\epsilon'|\epsilon) = N(\epsilon, 0.25)$. Because the proposal distribution is symmetric, this new value is accepted with probability

$$A = min\left(\frac{f(\epsilon')}{f(\epsilon)}, 1\right) \quad (8)$$

If the new value ϵ' has higher probability given T, k and δ under equation (6), it is accepted. If it has lower probability under equation (6), it is accepted at a rate corresponding to the ratio of its probability and the probability of the old value of ϵ.

After sampling ϵ, we resample δ with 10 iterations of Metropolis-Hastings. The proposal and acceptance functions are analogous to those for ϵ.

We ran multiple chains from different starting points to test convergence of T, ϵ, and δ. For the simulations reported below, we ran 1,000 iterations of Gibbs sampling. We took every tenth value from the last 500 iterations as samples from the posterior distribution over T, ϵ, and δ.

4 Data

We tested the model on a dataset selected from the CHILDES Treebank (Pearl and Sprouse, 2013). We used four corpora of child-directed speech (803,188 total words), which were parsed using the Charniak or Stanford parser and hand-checked by undergraduates. See Table 1 for corpus details.

Our dataset consists of sentences containing the 50 most frequent action verbs in these corpora that could be characterized as transitive, intransitive, or alternating. We excluded verbs that were obligatorily ditransitive or frequently took clausal or verbal complements: these included mental state verbs (e.g. *want*), aspectual verbs (e.g. *start*), modals (e.g. *should*), auxiliaries (e.g. *have*), and light verbs (e.g. *take*).

We sorted these 50 verbs into transitive, intransitive, and alternating categories according to the

Corpus	# Children	Ages	# Words	# Utterances
Brown- Adam, Eve, & Sarah, (Brown, 1973)	3	1;6-5;1	391,848	87,473
Soderstrom (Soderstrom et al., 2008)	2	0;6-1;0	90,608	24,130
Suppes (Suppes, 1974)	1	1;11-3;11	197,620	35,904
Valian (Valian, 1991)	21	1;9-2;8	123,112	25,551

Table 1: Corpora of Child-Directed Speech.

English verb classes described in Levin (1993), supplemented by our own intuitions for verbs not represented in that work. These classes provide a target for learning meant to align with adult speaker intuitions, independent of the corpus data that the model learns from. The transitive and intransitive categories are conservative; verbs like *jump* are considered alternating even though they occur infrequently in their possible transitive uses (e.g. *jump the horses over the fence*). These target categories thus set a high bar for our model to reach.

We then conducted an automated search over the Treebank trees for the total occurrences of each verb in the corpora, in all inflections, and the total occurrences with overt (pronounced) direct objects. These direct object counts included transitive basic clauses like those in (1), but not wh-object questions with object gaps like those in (3). Table 2 lists these 50 verbs along with their counts and percentage occurrences with direct objects.

Verb	Total	% DO
Transitive Verbs		
feed	222	0.93
fix	338	0.91
bring	606	0.89
throw	313	0.88
hit	215	0.87
buy	362	0.84
catch	185	0.76
hold	580	0.70
wear	477	0.60
Alternating Verbs		
pick	332	0.90
drop	169	0.88
lose	187	0.86
close	166	0.85
touch	183	0.84
leave	356	0.83
wash	196	0.82
pull	331	0.81
open	342	0.77
push	357	0.77
cut	263	0.75
turn	485	0.72
build	299	0.72
bite	197	0.72
knock	161	0.71
read	509	0.69

Verb	Total	% DO
Alternating Verbs, cont.		
break	553	0.63
drink	369	0.61
eat	1324	0.59
sing	307	0.52
blow	256	0.52
draw	376	0.51
move	241	0.46
ride	284	0.35
hang	153	0.35
stick	194	0.29
write	583	0.27
fit	229	0.21
play	1571	0.20
stand	301	0.07
run	230	0.06
swim	184	0.05
walk	253	0.04
jump	197	0.04
sit	862	0.01
Intransitive Verbs		
wait	383	0.15
work	256	0.04
cry	263	0.03
sleep	454	0.03
stay	308	0.01
fall	611	0.00

Table 2: Counts and percentage uses with direct objects (DO) of 50 verbs in dataset.

5 Simulations

We tested our model on the dataset described in the previous section. We compare our model's performance to an oracle model that already knows the parameters of the input filter, and two baselines.

5.1 Joint Inference Model

Figure 2 displays the posterior probability distributions over verb categories inferred by our joint inference model for each verb. Black bars represent the probability assigned to the transitive category, dark gray bars represent the probability assigned to the intransitive category, and light gray bars represent the probability assigned to the alternating category. The true categories for each verb are shown below the horizontal axis. Figure 3 displays the posterior distributions inferred for ϵ and δ.

The percentage of verbs categorized correctly by the model is reported in Table 3. The model achieves highest accuracy in categorizing the intransitive verbs: for all but one of these verbs, the model assigns highest probability to the intransitive category. The exception is the verb *wait*, which the model assigns highest probability under the alternating category. This is due to prevalent uses of temporal adjuncts, as in *wait a minute*, that were parsed as direct objects in the CHILDES Treebank. Thus, a learner who likewise misparses these adjuncts as direct objects would infer that *wait* is an alternating rather than intransitive verb.

The model assigns 6 out of the 9 transitive verbs highest probability under the transitive category. Three transitive verbs are assigned highest probability under the alternating rather than the transitive category: *catch, hold,* and *wear*. This is likely because these verbs display different behavior than the other transitive verbs in the corpus. The verb *hold* occurs frequently in verb-particle constructions (e.g. *hold on*), which might be treated differently than simple verbs by learners. The verbs *catch* and *wear* appear to occur at much higher rates than other transitive verbs in non-basic clauses: *catch* occurs frequently in passive constructions (e.g. *get caught*), and *wear* occurs frequently in

Figure 2: Posterior Distributions over Verb Categories (T), Joint Inference Model

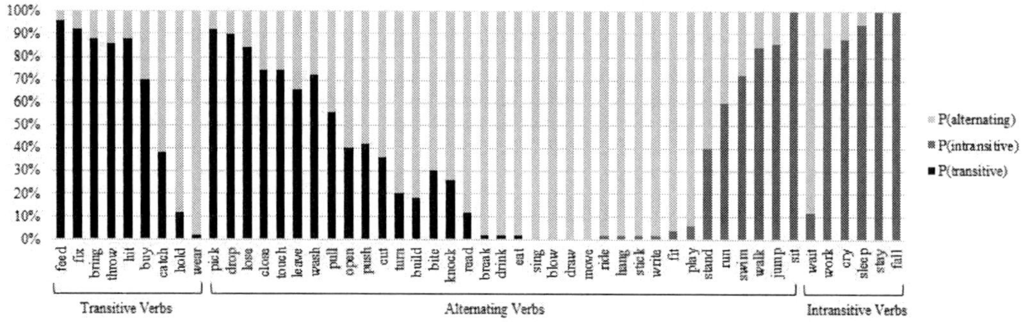

Figure 3: Posterior Distributions over ϵ and δ

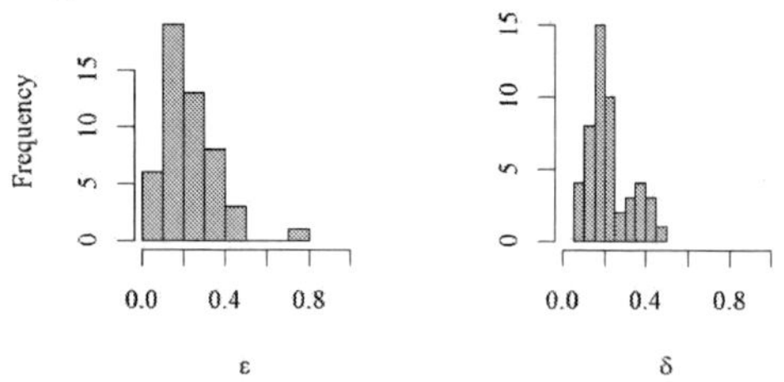

wh-object constructions (e.g. *what are you wearing?*). Whether learners likewise mis-classify these verbs, or can accommodate different rates of missing direct objects within the set of transitive verbs, is a topic for further investigation.

The model assigns highest probability for most of the alternating verbs to the alternating verb category. There are 13 exceptions. The verbs *pick, drop, lose, close, touch, leave, wash*, and *pull* are assigned highest probability under the transitive category because they infrequently occur in their possible intransitive uses in child-directed speech. The verbs *run, swim, walk, jump,* and *sit* are assigned highest probability under the intransitive category because these verbs very infrequently occur in their possible transitive uses. Thus, the model over-regularizes the alternating verbs that alternate infrequently, preferring the more deterministic transitive and intransitive verb categories.

In order to evaluate the model's inference of ϵ and δ, we estimated the true values of these parameters in our dataset. The proportion of transitive verbs with missing direct objects in the dataset gives us an estimate of $(1 - \delta) \times \epsilon$, and the proportion of intransitive verbs with spurious direct objects (e.g. *wait a minute*) gives us an estimate of $\delta \times \epsilon$. Solving these two equations, we find that $\delta = 0.18$ and $\epsilon = 0.24$. The posterior probability distribution over δ inferred by our model has a mean of 0.23, and the probability distribution over ϵ has a mean of 0.22. Our model thus slightly over-estimates the value of δ and under-estimates the value of ϵ. However, it infers values for these parameters close to the true values in the corpus, enabling it to infer the correct transitivity properties for 2/3 of the verbs in our dataset.

5.2 Oracle Model

To evaluate our model's performance, we compare it against an oracle model in which δ is fixed to 0.18 and ϵ to 0.24 in order to reflect their estimated true values in our dataset. This allows us to see how our model compares to a model that knows the parameters for the input filter in advance.

The posterior probability distributions over verb categories inferred by the oracle model are displayed in Figure 4. Our joint inference model performs identically to the oracle model with intransitive verbs, and almost as well with transitive verbs: the oracle model succeeds in identifying one more transitive verb, *catch*, as transitive. Our joint inference model performs better than the oracle model in categorizing alternating verbs: the oracle model has an even higher tendency to over-regularize the verbs that alternate infrequently.

Inferring the parameters of the input filter thus results in comparable, and maybe slightly better, accuracy in categorizing verbs than knowing these parameters in advance. It should be noted that the values of these parameters are important: when we run a version of the oracle model with inappropriate values for ϵ and δ, performance decreases substantially. Thus, our model performs comparably to

Model	% Transitive	% Intransitive	% Alternating	% Total Verbs
Joint Inference	0.67	0.83	0.63	0.66
Oracle	0.77	0.83	0.54	0.62
No-Filter Baseline	0.00	0.00	1.00	0.70
Random Baseline	0.33	0.33	0.34	0.34

Table 3: Percentages of Verbs Categorized Correctly.

Figure 4: Posterior Distributions over Verb Categories (T), Oracle Model

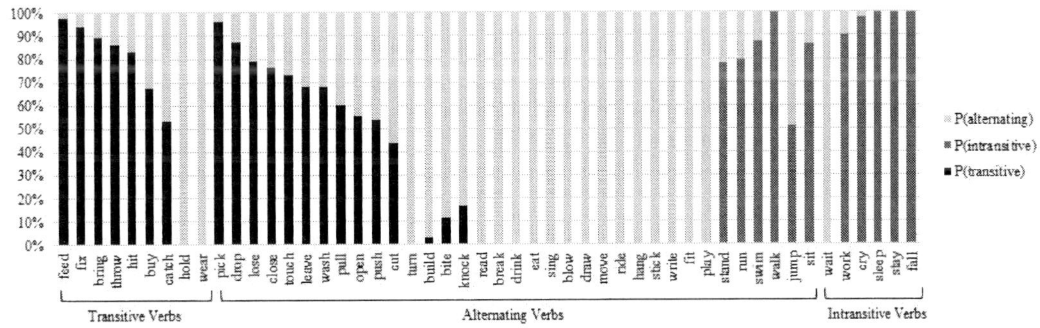

the best-case oracle model not merely because it infers an input filter, but because it infers the best parameters for such a filter given our dataset.

5.3 No-Filter Baseline

We've seen that our model accurately categorizes 2/3 of the verbs in our dataset by inferring appropriate parameters of a filter on its input, and performs comparably overall with a model that knows those parameters in advance. To determine how much the input filter matters in this inference, we compare our model to a baseline that lacks this filter. We can instantiate a model with no filter by setting ϵ to zero, representing zero probability of parsing errors. Because every verb in our dataset occurs some but not all of the time with direct objects, and this model assumes there are no parsing errors to filter out, it assigns every verb to the alternating category. It thus categorizes 100% of the alternating verbs correctly, achieving 70% overall accuracy because alternating verbs make up 70% of our dataset. However, this accuracy comes at the cost of failing to categorize any verbs as transitive or intransitive. Our joint inference model performs substantially better in this regard, categorizing the majority of transitive and intransitive verbs correctly. Thus, an input filter is important for differentiating alternating from non-alternating verbs.

5.4 Random Baseline

We finally compare our model against a baseline that assigns verbs randomly to transitivity categories, assuming that each value of T has equal prior probability. For each verb in our dataset this model flips a fair 3-sided coin to determine its transitivity category. This model thus categorizes 1/3 of the transitive, intransitive, and alternating verbs correctly, resulting in 34% overall accuracy. Our joint inference model performs significantly better on each verb class, and nearly twice as well overall.

5.5 Summary

We find that inferring an appropriate filter on the input matters for verb transitivity learning, but that the parameters of this input filter can be learned. Our model performs comparably to an oracle model that knows these values in advance. It performs substantially better in categorizing transitive and intransitive verbs than a baseline model that lacks an input filter altogether, and performs twice as well overall as a random baseline. These results demonstrate that our model is able to infer reasonable values for the input filter parameters, allowing it to accurately categorize the majority of transitive, intransitive, and alternating verbs.

6 Discussion

In this paper we introduce a model that infers the parameters of a filter on its input for argument structure acquisition. Our model accurately categorizes 2/3 of the most frequent transitive, intransitive, and alternating verbs in child-directed speech on the basis of their distributions with and without direct objects, by learning to filter out sentences that were likely mis-parsed. This enables the learner to avoid drawing faulty inferences about verb transitivity from non-basic clause types, such as wh-object questions, that may be mistaken for intransitive clauses. Our model performs substantially better than baseline models that lack an input filter and performs comparably to an oracle model that knows these input filter parameters in advance, demonstrating that this input filter both matters for verb learning and can be learned.

Our model offers a novel solution to the problem of identifying an appropriate input filter for verb learning (Lidz and Gleitman, 2004; Pinker, 1984) : where previous approaches have implicitly assumed that children must have a way of identifying the sentences to be filtered, our model learns an input filter without knowing its parameters in advance. Instead, the learner infers the input filter parameters jointly with verb transitivity. This reduces the prior knowledge needed for initial verb learning: the child does not need to identify which sentences likely contain wh-questions and other non-basic clause types as a prerequisite for learning which verbs are transitive. Note that we do not claim that the Bayesian joint inference performed by our model represents the exact algorithms performed by child learners; although there is substantial literature on young children's statistical inference capabilities (Gomez and Gerken, 2000), this model is intended only as a proof of concept that such joint inference is possible.

The model makes two types of errors in inferring verb categories. First, it is unable to correctly categorize some transitive and intransitive verbs that behave differently than other verbs in their category, such as *catch, hold, wear*, and *wait*. Further investigation is necessary to determine whether these verbs pose difficulties for child learners as well. A second type of error is over-regularizing alternating verbs that alternate infrequently: the model prefers to assign these verbs to the transitive and intransitive categories. This is an example of a learner preferring a more deterministic analysis for probabilistic input, a tendency also found in child learners in artificial language studies (Hudson Kam and Newport, 2009). The error-filtering mechanism we present here could thus potentially provide a way to model other forms of over-regularization in learning.

Other future directions include extending this model to cross-linguistic data, particularly to languages with free object-drop. Chinese, Korean, and Japanese have a syntactic mechanism for dropping the direct object of any transitive verb, unlike in English where object-drop is a lexical property of specific verbs. As as result, learners of these languages might be subject to even higher rates of parsing errors if they perceive object-drop sentences as intransitive. For this reason, these languages are potentially problematic for syntactic bootstrapping strategies that rely on learners accurately identifying transitive verbs (Lee and Naigles, 2005; Lee and Naigles, 2008). But if appropriate parameters for filtering out problematic object-drop constructions in these languages can be inferred, our model may help address concerns with the feasibility of syntactic bootstrapping in these languages.

Finally, this model learns verb transitivity by effectively filtering out sentences containing non-basic clause types, without identifying what these clause types are. But children do eventually learn to identify non-basic constructions in their language. If children initially filter out certain sentences as parsing errors for the purposes of verb learning, they must eventually learn that many of these sentences are generated by systematic syntactic operations, such as those that create wh-questions in English. In future work, we aim to investigate whether a learner can identify which non-basic constructions are present in sentences that were parsed in error. Learning verb transitivity can likely help the child identify these constructions: if a child expects a direct object for a verb and encounters sentences where this object does not appear, that child may be compelled to examine those anomalous sentences to determine the cause of the missing object. Thus, a strategy of filtering out non-basic constructions by initially treating them as parsing errors may eventually help the learner identify not only verb transitivity, but also the nature of those non-basic constructions themselves.

Acknowledgments We gratefully acknowledge the support of NSF grant BCS-1551629 and NSF NRT award DGE-1449815. We would also like to thank the UMD ProbMod reading group and CNL Lab for their helpful discussions.

References

Frans Adriaans and Daniel Swingley. 2012. Distributional learning of vowel categories is supported by prosody in infant-directed speech. *Proceedings of the 34th Annual Conference of the Cognitive Science Society*, pages 72–77.

Afra Alishahi and Suzanne Stevenson. 2008. A computational model of early argument structure acquisition. *Cognitive Science*, 32:789834.

Roger Brown. 1973. *A First Language: The Early Stages*. Harvard University Press, Cambridge, MA.

Noam Chomsky. 1965. *Aspects of the theory of syntax*. MIT Press, Cambridge, MA.

Noam Chomsky. 1981. *Lectures on government and binding*. Foris Publications.

Cynthia Fisher, Yael Gertner, Rose M. Scott, and Sylvia Yuan. 2010. Syntactic bootstrapping. *Wiley Interdisciplinary Reviews: Cognitive Science*, 1(2):143–149.

Annie Gagliardi, Tara M. Mease, and Jeffrey Lidz. 2016. Discontinuous development in the acquisition of filler-gap dependencies: Evidence from 15-and 20-month-olds. *Language Acquisition*, 23(3):1–27.

Stuart Geman and Donald Geman. 1984. Stochastic relaxation, Gibbs distributions, and the Bayesian restoration of images. *IEEE-PAMI*, 6:721–741.

Lila R. Gleitman. 1990. The structural sources of verb meanings. *Language acquisition*, 1(1):3–55.

Rebecca L. Gomez and LouAnn Gerken. 2000. Infant artificial language learning and language acquisition. *Trends in Cognitive Sciences*, 4(5):178–186.

Jane Grimshaw. 1990. *Argument Structure*. MIT Press, Cambridge, MA.

W. K. Hastings. 1970. Monte Carlo sampling methods using Markov chains and their applications. *Biometrika*, 57(1):97–109.

Carla L. Hudson Kam and Elissa L. Newport. 2009. Getting it right by getting it wrong: When learners change languages. *Cognitive Psychology*, 59:30–66.

Barbara Landau and Lila R. Gleitman. 1985. *Language and Experience: Evidence from the Blind Child*. Harvard University Press.

Howard Lasnik. 1989. On certain substitutes for negative data. In Robert J. Matthews and William Demopoulos, editors, *Learnability and linguistic theory*, pages 89–105. Kluwer, Dordrecht.

Joanne N. Lee and Letitia R. Naigles. 2005. The input to verb learning in mandarin chinese: A role for syntactic bootstrapping. *Developmental Psychology*, 41(3):529–540.

Joanne N. Lee and Letitia R. Naigles. 2008. Mandarin learners use syntactic bootstrapping in verb acquisition. *Cognition*, 106(2):1028–1037.

Beth Levin. 1993. *English Verb Classes and Alternations: A Preliminary Investigation*. University of Chicago Press, Chicago, IL.

Jeffrey Lidz and Lila R. Gleitman. 2004. Yes, we still need Universal Grammar. *Cognition*, 94:85–93.

Lisa Pearl and Jeffrey Lidz. 2009. When domain-general learning fails and when it succeeds: Identifying the contribution of domain specificity. *Language Learning and Development*, 5:235–265.

Lisa Pearl and Jon Sprouse. 2013. Syntactic islands and learning biases: Combining experimental syntax and computational modeling to investigate the language acquisition problem. *Language Acquisition*, 20(1):23–68.

Amy Perfors, Joshua B. Tenenbaum, and Elizabeth Wonnacott. 2010. Variability, negative evidence, and the acquisition of verb argument constructions. *Journal of Child Language*, 37:607–642.

Steven Pinker. 1984. *Language Learnability and Language Development*. Cambridge, MA: Harvard University Press.

Steven Pinker. 1989. *Learnability and Cognition: The Acquisition ofArgument Structure*. Cambridge, MA: MIT Press.

Melanie Soderstrom, Megan Blossom, Irena Foygel, and James L. Morgan. 2008. Acoustical cues and grammatical units in speech to two preverbal infants. *Journal of Child Language*, 35:869–902.

Karen Stromswold. 1995. The Acquisition of Subject and Object Wh-questions. *Language Acquisition*, 4(1/2):5–48.

Patrick Suppes. 1974. The semantics of children's language. *American Psychologist*, 29:103–114.

Virginia Valian. 1991. Syntactic subjects in the early speech of American and Italian children. *Cognition*, 40(1-2):21–81.

Grounding sound change in ideal observer models of perception

Zachary J. Burchill
Dept. of Brain & Cognitive Sciences
University of Rochester
zburchil@ur.rochester.edu

T. Florian Jaeger
Dept. of Brain & Cognitive Sciences
University of Rochester
fjaeger@ur.rochester.edu

Abstract

An important predictor of historical sound change, functional load, fails to capture insights from speech perception. Building on ideal observer models of word recognition, we devise a new definition of functional load that incorporates both *a priori* expectedness and perceptual information. We explore this new measure with a simple model and find that it outperforms traditional measures.

1 Introduction

Whether a phonemic contrast (e.g., /t/ vs /d/) merges over historical time has been taken to depend on its **functional load**—essentially its utility in distinguishing different meanings (Gilliéron, 1918; Jakobson, 1931; Malthesius, 1931). Traditionally, functional load is operationalized as the number of minimal pair words distinguished only by the contrast (e.g., for the /t/-/d/ contrast, the words *ten* and *den*). Studies based on this measure have found higher functional load to be associated with lowered likelihood of merging (Wedel et al., 2013). However, traditional measures of functional load fail to capture important properties from speech perception that are critical if one seeks to understand how a phonological contrast adds to word identification in actual language use. Specifically, research on speech perception has found that the functional contribution of phonemic contrasts to word identification depends on:

i. the *degree* to which the contrast is perceptually distinguishable,

ii. the *degree* to which the contrast gradiently adds to the distinction between *any* pair of words, not only minimal pairs,

iii. the *interaction* of (i) and (ii): how the perceptual distinguishability affects word recognition depends on the word's specific phonological neighbors.

Building on ideal observer models of spoken word recognition such as Norris and McQueen (2008) and similarly, Luce and Pisoni (1998), we integrate (i)-(iii) into a revised definition of functional load. We then evaluate this novel definition empirically.

2 Theoretical model

In order to understand the amount of "work" a contrast does, we first seek to understand the implications of *losing* the contrast. Traditionally functional load is thought of as the number of meaning distinctions lost when a contrast disappears. Our revised definition measures functional load as the overall decrease in *probability* of correctly recognizing meaning. We measure functional load by first calculating the confusion in the system with the contrast in place, then, merging the contrast in question, re-calculate the confusion of the system without the contrast and measure the difference. For the present purpose, we follow previous work and operationalize meanings as lexical entries (or short, words). Thus:

$$FL_c = \text{E}[\text{p}(\text{CorrectWordRecognition}_{\text{with c}})] - \text{E}[\text{p}(\text{CorrectWordRecognition}_{\text{without c}})] \quad (1)$$

Equation (1) defines functional load as the expected value (i.e. the mean) of the probability of correct word recognition when the system has the contrast c minus the expected value for the same language without the contrast. In this paper we entertain two conceptualizations for the expected value: one for which each word/meaning type is equally important (which we shall refer to as *type-based* functional load) and one in which words are weighted by their relative frequencies (*token-based* functional load).

Proceedings of the 7th Workshop on Cognitive Modeling and Computational Linguistics (CMCL 2017), pages 20–28,
Valencia, Spain, April 7, ©2017 Association for Computational Linguistics

Taking context into account, the type-based expected value of the probability of recognizing a word (i.e.: $\mathrm{E}[\mathrm{p}(CorrectWordRecognition)]$) would be equivalent to taking the average of the probabilities of recognizing all words in the lexicon, i.e.:

$$\frac{\sum_{w_s}^{L} f(\mathrm{p}(w_h|w_s, ctxt))}{|L|} \quad (2)$$

where L is the set of word types in the lexicon, w_s is the word spoken by the talker, w_h is the word heard by the interlocutor, and $ctxt$ is the context the word was spoken in. f is a function of the choice rule that determines $\mathrm{p}(w_h = w_s|w_s, ctxt)$ from the distribution of all potentially heard words, $\mathrm{p}(w_h|w_s, ctxt)$. For example, f could be the *criterion rule* (Green and Swets, 1966) whereby the probability of the listener correctly recognizing the word is calculated as the probability that the intended word has the highest chance of being heard out of all other candidates.

Token-based functional load can be formulated similarly, but instead of merely averaging the probabilities of recognizing each word, one takes the weighted average, where each probability is weighted by the word's frequency:

$$\frac{\sum_{w_s}^{L} \mathrm{p}(w_s|ctxt) \cdot \mathrm{p}(ctxt) \cdot f(\mathrm{p}(w_h|w_s, ctxt))}{\sum_{w_s}^{L} \mathrm{p}(w_s|ctxt) \cdot \mathrm{p}(ctxt)} \quad (3)$$

These two approaches make different claims about the pressures on language change—token-based accounts imply that the average number of misrecognitions exerts the pressure, whereas type-based accounts would suggest the number of meanings confused is most important. Similar distinctions have been made previously, for example, Martinet (1952) and Hockett (1955) argue that lexical frequency should affect functional load, similar to how we weigh probabilities of recognition in our token-based account. Conceivably, either approach might better capture how languages change, or perhaps some higher-level utility function weighs words' relative importance (e.g., words that have greater utility in recognizing contribute more). One of the benefits of our modeling approach is that we can quantitatively compare the two accounts.

Our proposal shares with entropic accounts (Hockett, 1967; Surendran and Niyogi, 2003; Surendran and Niyogi, 2006) that it incorporates the *probability* of recognizing words (via contextual predictability). However, the present proposal also incorporates perceptual confusability. On the other hand, ideal observer models predict that word recognition depends on both perceptual distinguishability and contextual predictability (capturing both bottom-up and top-down influences on word recognition). We therefore estimate $f(\mathrm{p}(w_h = w_i|w_i, ctxt))$, the probability of correctly recognizing word w_i, by comparing the *perceptual* confusability of w_i with all other words in the lexicon, weighted by frequency, following Luce and Pisoni (1998).

3 Approach

3.1 Estimating word recognition rates

Although contextual predictability could be included in future versions of our model, we ignore it for simplicity's sake, essentially approximating rates of isolated word recognition. We calculate the predicted probability of recognizing an isolated word w_i as:

$$\frac{\text{PerceptualConfusability}(w_i, w_i) \cdot \log Freq_i}{\sum_{j \in L} \text{PerceptualConfusability}(w_j, w_i) \cdot \log Freq_j} \quad (4)$$

where the L is the set of all word forms in the lexicon (i.e. pairwise calculations with w_i and every other word form, w_j, including itself). The general formulation of Equation (4) follows Luce and Pisoni (1998), using Luce's choice rule—i.e. hearing each word out of all the alternatives at a probability equal to the probability that particular word (Luce, 1959). In essence, the numerator is a measure of how likely the listener is to hear the phones in w_i correctly, weighted by frequency of w_i. The denominator is the frequency-weighted sum of the probabilities of mishearing the phones in w_i as all other possible words.

We estimate the perceptual confusability of two strings of phones, $\text{PerceptualConfusability}(x_j, x_i)$, as the product of the probabilities of confusing phones in the first string (x_i) with phones at the same locations in the second string (x_j), using probabilities from a phoneme-to-phoneme confusion matrix we built with perceptual data collected from Cutler et al. (2004).

$$\text{PerceptualConfusability}(x_j, x_i) = \prod_{a=1}^{n} \text{P}(p_{aj}|p_{ai}) \quad (5)$$

where n is the number of phones in x_i and $\text{P}(p_{aj}|p_{ai})$ represents the conditional probability of hearing the ath phone in x_i (p_{ai}) as the ath phone in x_j (p_{aj}). The formulation of Equation (5) currently entails that we are only considering words of equal length to the target when calculating perceptual confusion. Future work can consider deletion and insertion confusions (Levy, 2008).

With the phonological data from the CMU Pronouncing Dictionary (Weide, 1998) and lexical frequencies collected from the SUBTLEX-US frequency database (Brysbaert and New, 2009), we can estimate the probability of correctly recognizing over 42,000 word forms of American English. The recognition rates predicted by this method have been shown to mirror properties of spoken word recognition (Luce and Pisoni, 1998). Combining these data, we can calculate $\text{E}[\text{p}(CorrectWordRecognition_{\text{with c}})]$ from (1).

3.2 Simulating contrast loss

The perceptual confusion matrix our model uses can be considered an estimate of the perceptual distinguishability of all phonemes in English as it exists currently. To simulate a hypothetical version of English that *does not* contain a certain contrast, we can artificially manipulate the confusion matrix our model uses to make the phonemes in the contrast perceptually indistinguishable.

For example, to simulate a variety in English in which there is no longer a distinction between /t/ and /d/, we can redistribute the probability mass of the confusion matrix so that p(/t/$_{heard}$|/d/$_{spoken}$) = p(/t/$_{heard}$|/t/$_{spoken}$) and vice versa (Figure 1). The probability that a listener would recognize a /t/ as a /t/ would then be equal to the probability they recognize the phoneme as a /d/. Combining this altered confusion matrix with (4), we can rerun our model, calculating the average probability of correctly recognizing words without the contrast, and estimate $\text{E}[\text{p}(CorrectWordRecognition_{\text{without c}})]$.

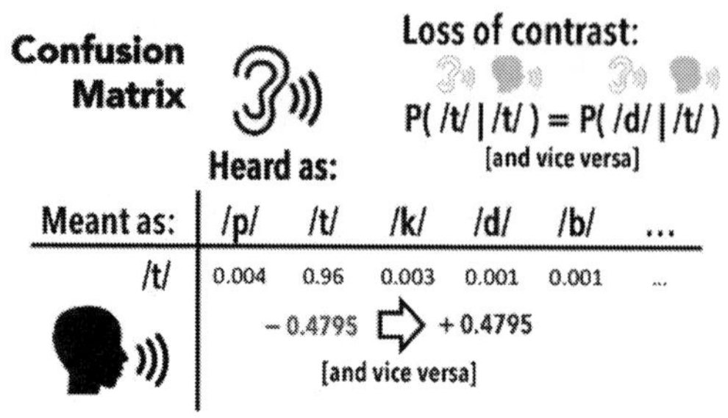

Figure 1: Manipulating the probability mass in the phoneme-to-phoneme confusion matrix to simulate losing the /t/-/d/ contrast.

4 Verifying our model's properties

Earlier, we stated that a definition of functional load that captures what is known about spoken word recognition should depend on (i)-(iii). In the follow sections, we verify that our model captures these properties (though under simplifying assumptions).

4.1 Revised functional load depends on contrasts' *a priori* perceptual distinguishability

Phonemes differ in their ease of recognition and differentiation acoustically and perceptually (Miller and Nicely, 1955; Wang and Bilger, 1973; Cutler et al., 2004). Some phonemes are harder to correctly recognize than others, and some contrasts are more readily confused. The loss of a phonemic contrast with high *a priori* perceptual confusability will affect word recognition less than losing a contrast between two very perceptually distinct phonemes, all other things being equal. For example, the /ɑ/-/ɔ/ contrast in American English has low perceptual distinguishability, even in non-merging dialects (Cutler et al., 2004). Losing this contrast increased predicted misrecognition rates by 6.6%. In comparison, removal of the same contrast in a simulated version of English where /ɑ/-/ɔ/ are highly distinct (i.e., the original confusability reduced by 80%) increased misrecognition rates by 10.1%.

4.2 Contrast loss affects more than just minimal pairs

Traditional functional load—including recent extensions (Surendran and Niyogi, 2006; Wedel et al., 2013)—fail to capture the fact that real-world

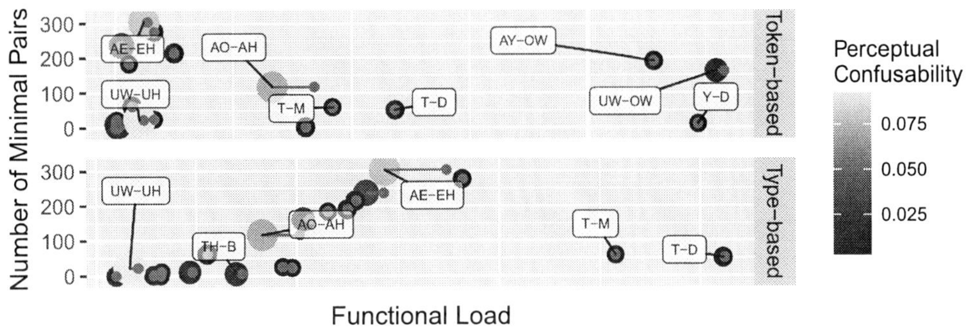

Figure 2: Twenty randomly chosen mergers demonstrating the complex relationship of perception, phonotactics, and the lexicon (with Arpabet labels). Size and color of dots indicate the *a priori* perceptual confusability of the contrast, as estimated by the original confusion matrix. Axes are scaled independently. The red lines show the increase in the contrast's functional load had the contrast originally been perfectly perceptually distinct—in essence, the sensitivity of the contrast's functional load to its *a priori* confusability.

spoken word recognition is influenced by word-to-word confusability beyond the confusability of minimal pairs. For example, the perceptual confusability of pairs like /gɑt/ and /cɔt/ will never be taken into account, yet these two words are likely to be relatively confusable, even in American dialects that preserve the /ɑ/-/ɔ/ distinction. Following a /g/-/k/ merger, /gɑt/ and /cɔt/ would not be completely indistinguishable, but the two words would be *highly* confusable.

Our approach compares the perceptual distinguishability of each word and *all* other words in the lexicon (the present implementation: all words with the same number of phonemes), avoiding this problem. To illustrate how this changes the operationalization of functional load, we compared token-based functional load of the /g/-/k/ contrast under two different assumptions: one in which only minimal pairs were considered neighbors and one in which all the words in the lexicon were considered. When our model only used minimal pairs as neighbors (i.e. for each w_i in (4), L was restricted to w_i and its /g/-/k/ minimal pairs), words containing /g/ or /k/ had a mean probability of misrecognition of 0.023; when the model used all non-minimal pair neighbors of the same length (as we do in the rest of this paper), misrecognition increased to a probability of 0.064, corresponding to a three-fold increase in odds.

4.3 Functional load depends on a complex interaction of elements

Our definition of functional load does predicts interactions between a contrast's perceptual distinguishability and its distribution across words and neighbors in the lexicon. In this section, we first highlight the differences in predictions between our type- and token-based accounts. We then demonstrate how perceptual confusability, distribution of the phones in the lexicon, and the interactions between the two are predicted to affect functional load. Figure (2) demonstrates the outcomes of these complex relationships for 20 randomly chosen phonemic contrasts. Both type- and token-based functional load are plotted against the number of minimal pairs formed by each contrast. The red lines represent how sensitive that contrast's functional load is to *a priori* perceptual con fusability. The red dots represent a contrast's functional load, had its phones been completely perceptually distinguishable to begin with. In general, we would expect that contrasts with low *a priori* perceptual confusability would be less sensitive to eliminating this confusability, as they are already closer to perfect distinguishability.

We see first that type- and token-based accounts of functional load differ noticeably in their estimates of functional load. Figure (2) shows a fairly linear relationship between type-based functional load and the traditional measure, and although this relationship becomes less clear with

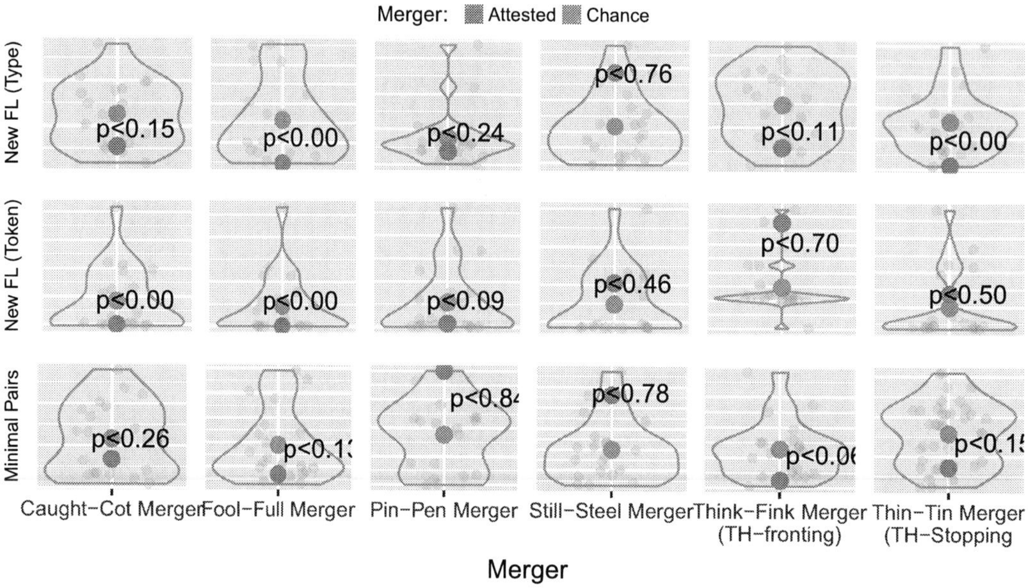

Figure 3: The functional loads of six attested mergers in North American English each compared to 20 randomly generated mergers in the same environments, measured by models implementing our new definition of functional load vs. the traditional measure of number of minimal pairs. The probability that a sample drawn from the distribution of random mergers has less than or equal functional load than the attested merger is indicated. Axes are scaled independently for each plot.

more contrasts (not pictured), the token-based account is noticeably less correlated with the number of minimal pairs. This difference makes sense: type-based functional load and the number of minimal pairs a contrast separates both emphasize word types. However, it also serves as a demonstration that lexical-phonological environments are not generally uniform across words of different frequencies–further evidence that choosing between type- vs. token- approaches should be a matter of careful consideration (Hockett, 1955; Martinet, 1952; Wedel et al., 2013).

Secondly, there are contrasts whose functional loads seem to be determined more by their initial perceptual distinguishability, or possibly by how they are distributed across non-minimal pair neighbors. Although the /t/-/m/ contrast does not separate many minimal pairs, the type-based account predicts that a merger would be unlikely, possibly due to the low *a priori* perceptual confusability of the phones. A benefit of our model is that it allows the researcher to ask questions about how the lexicon and phonological system interact; exactly how these contribute to a contrast's functional load can be teased apart.

Third, although the functional loads of naturally confusable contrasts are generally more sensitive to perceptual changes, there are exceptions to this pattern. For example, the functional load for the most perceptually confusable contrast, /u/-/ʊ/ ("UW-UH" in Figure 2), hardly increases at all when the original contrast is made less confusable. Even if this phonemic contrast were conveyed with perfect clarity, it would not drastically change how accurately words are recognized. This suggests that the functional load of the /u/-/ʊ/ contrast is more a product of its distribution in the lexicon than its perceptual confusability.

Finally, type- and token-based accounts also vary in how sensitive the functional load of their contrasts are to their *a priori* perceptual confusability. For example, the /æ/-/ɛ/ contrast ("AE-EH" in Figure 2), has high *a priori* perceptual confusability. The token-based functional load of this contrast increases only slightly when the contrast is made perfectly perceptually distinct, demonstrating a relative robustness to initial perceptual confusability. However, the type-based functional load of the same contrast shows the *most* sensitivity to initial perceptual confusability. The fact that the weighting of lexical frequency can modulate how perceptual contributions affect our model's functional load suggests that in addition to capturing the impact of perceptual and lexical factors impact individually, our model also captures their interactions.

5 Evaluating our new definition

Although our definition of functional load has been built on a model of spoken word recognition that is known to work well in predicting human data (Luce and Pisoni, 1998), the question has been left open of whether this operationalization is actually a good predictor of sound change. If the previously observed effects of functional load on sound change are indeed relevant to a contrast's functional contribution to spoken word recognition, then we expect that models such as ours should be successful in predicting mergers.

In order to evaluate performance, we compare the functional load of actual attested mergers with randomly chosen phonological mergers in similar environments. The logic here is that the if high functional load prevents mergers[1], we would expect to see that attested mergers have significantly less functional load than random hypothetical mergers.

5.1 Methods

To get the most accurate sense of a merger's functional load, we need to calculate it in the environment of the language in which it is taking place. Because our model is based on American English, we limit ourselves to mergers that are currently taking place in varieties of American English. The attested vowel mergers here represent the four most attested vowel mergers in North America (Labov et al., 2006)[2]: the *caught-cot* merger (also known as the "low back merger") is a environment-independent (in this model) merger of /ɑ/ and /ɔ/. The *fool-full* merger merges /u/ and /ʊ/ before /l/, the *pin-pen* merger merges /ɪ/-/ɛ/ before nasals, and the *still-steel* merger merges /ɪ/-/i/ before /l/. Consonant mergers in English are much more rare, and the consonant mergers here represent the two most straightforward attested mergers in varieties of American English we could find. The "think-fink" merger (*th-fronting*) merges dental fricatives and labiodental fricatives, and the "thin-tin" merger (*th-stopping*) merges dental fricatives and dental plosives.

To compare the functional load of attested mergers with random mergers, we compare each attested merger with 20 randomly chosen phonological mergers that take place in the same phonetic environments as the attested mergers. For example, the *pin-pen merger* merges /ɪ/-/ɛ/ before nasals; to compare, we chose 20 random vowel contrasts and merged them before nasals as well. The contrasts in the hypothetical mergers were chosen by randomly sampling all possible pairings of phonemes, the only constraint being that only vowels were considered for comparison to attested vowel mergers and only consononants for the attested consonant mergers[3].

Using a kernel density estimate calculated from the distribution of random mergers, we calculate the probability that a sample drawn from the distribution of theoretically possible similar mergers would have a functional load less than or equal to that of the attested merger. Attested mergers should have lower functional load than theoretical mergers, as they have actually happened in various dialects of American English. Figure (3) compares our models to a traditional measure, the number of minimal pairs erased by a contrast.

5.2 Results

As shown in Figure (3), both of our models outperform the traditional measure for at least four of the six mergers. The type-based model predicts each attested merger relatively well: with the exception of the *still-steel* merger (which no measure was able to predict), the type-based model predicts each attested merger with at least $p<0.3$. Although the token-based model performs relatively well for the rest of the six, *TH-stopping* and *TH-fronting* have higher-than-average token-based functional loads compared to the random mergers. The only merger the number of minimal pairs predicts better than both of our mod-

[1]Low functional load *driving* mergers and high functional load *preventing* mergers are two separate hypotheses. In practice, they are hard to distinguish, and doing so is not the purpose of the current paper. Rather, we seek to assess whether our functional load measure is a good predictor of mergers compared to the standard notion.

[2]Labov et al. (2006) also mention that there is preliminary evidence for five more possible mergers in North American English before /l/, but note that these require further study.

[3]Limiting the comparison to, say, only mergers that are attested in other languages, would have introduced elements of cirularity into the logic of our test. It is possible that contrasts have merged *because* they have low functional load to begin with.

els is for *TH-fronting*, and its performance over the type-based model is relatively small ($p<0.06$ vs. $p<0.11$). Both of our models predict the attested mergers better numerically than the traditional measure for all four of the vowel mergers, though for the *still-steel* merger the type-based model and the traditional measure are practically identical ($p<0.76$ vs. $p<0.78$).

The difference is less clear when comparing the type- and token-based models. Numerically, the token-based model outperforms the type-based model on the *caught-cot*, *pin-pen*, and *still-steel* mergers, but for these mergers, the type-based model still does relatively well ($p<0.15$ for the *caught-cot* merger and $p<0.24$ for the *pin-pen* merger) or both models do poorly (for the *still-steel* merger, token: $p<0.46$ vs type: $p<0.78$). For the two mergers where the type-based model predicts the attested mergers better than the token-based model, it makes relatively accurate predictions while the token-based model does not predict the merger (for *TH-fronting*: $p<0.11$ vs. $p<0.70$, and for *TH-stopping*: $p<0.00$ vs. $p<0.50$). This could suggest that the type-based account of functional load better captures the pressures of sound change, but further testing is be required to make a more definitive comparison.

6 Discussion

As more studies highlight the relationships between the lexicon, perceptual information, and language change (Ohala, 1993b; Ohala, 1993a; Hall, 2009; Hall et al., submitted; Kang and Cohen, 2016), some have found that incorporating perceptual data into accounts of functional load can succeed where traditional measures cannot (Tsui, 2012). In this paper, we have incorporated key insights from speech perception with ideal observer models of word recognition to form a revised definition of functional load. Implementing this definition with a simple model, we find that it outperforms the traditional measure of functional load, and gives us new insight into the process of language change.

For example, the type-based model's better confidence in predicting attested mergers compared to the token-based model tentatively suggests that misrecognizing meaning *types* exerts more pressure on sound change than the average number of times one misrecognizes words (i.e. according to the frequency with which one encounters them). These results are in line with Wedel et al. (2013), insofar both argue against the claim from Martinet (1952) that functional load should be determined by weighing words' functional contribution with their frequencies.

6.1 Future directions

We close by briefly discussing the simplifying assumptions of the present model, and how they can be addressed in future work. In the current study, perceptual confusability between two phonemes is calculated from a phoneme-to-phoneme confusion matrix, which simplifies phoneme recognition considerably. Unlike the smaller data set in (Luce and Pisoni, 1998), the data from (Cutler et al., 2004) was collected through a forced-choice task, with participants hearing only VC and CV syllables, and being only able to respond in kind. Although less constrained studies could offer more sophisticated behavioral data (e.g. including consonant clusters, etc.), experimentally collecting so much data can quickly become onerous.

The benefits of using acoustic/perceptual information also go beyond what has been covered in the current paper. For instance, it is worth noting that in all previous conceptions of functional load, phonological mergers have always been viewed as detrimental to recognition or to separating meanings, etc. However, when considering how sound change could affect actual spoken message transmission, we realize that mergers could in theory *benefit* communication. Imagine for example, a phone that is important to communication–but easily confused with another important phone–merges with a relatively unimportant phone. If the process of merging moves the phone in question acoustically (and perceptually) away from its confusable competitor, then the gain in recognition could in theory outweigh the loss from merging. In short, not all mergers of a phonemic contrast are equal: the direction in which a contrast merges should impact the system differently. Our model can thus in principle be used to make predictions of about the specific acoustic outcome of merges, and these predictions can be tested against data. For example, in the *pin-pen* merger, the result of the merger is generally closer to /ɪ/ than /ɛ/. Does this direction have a lower functional load than a merger in the opposite direction?

Additionally, ideal observer models predict word recognition based on contextual predictability—although we ignore contextual predictability in this paper, it would be relatively straight forward to incorporate it in future versions of the model, for example, via measures of average predictability. Additionally, the model in the current paper analyzes *isolated* spoken word recognition. In the future, we could estimate word recognition in the context of sentences by incorporating n-gram frequencies from conversational corpora into the model.

7 Acknowledgments

We would like to thank our three anonymous reviewers for their incredibly helpful feedback and suggestions in revising this paper.

References

Marc Brysbaert and Boris New. 2009. Moving beyond Kučera and Francis: A. critical evaluation of current word frequency norms and the introduction of a new and improved word frequency measure for American English. *Behavior research methods*, 41(4):977–990.

Anne Cutler, Andrea Weber, Roel Smits, and Nicole Cooper. 2004. Patterns of English phoneme confusions by native and non-native listeners. *The Journal of the Acoustical Society of America*, 116(6):3668–3678.

Jules Gilliéron. 1918. *G.énéalogie des mots qui désignent l'abeille d'après l'Atlas linguistique de la France*, volume 225. É.. Champion, Paris.

D. M. Green and J. A. Swets. 1966. *Signal detection theory and psychophysics*. Robert E. Krieger Publishing Co., Huntington, NY.

Kathleen Currie Hall, Elizabeth Hume, T. Florian Jaeger, and Andrew Wedel. submitted. The message shapes phonology.

Kathleen Currie Hall. 2009. *A probabilistic model of phonological relationships from contrast to allophony*. Ph.D. thesis, The Ohio State University.

Charles Francis Hockett. 1955. *A manual of phonology*. Waverly Press.

Charles Francis Hockett. 1967. The quantification of functional load. *Word*, 23(1-3):300–320.

Roman Jakobson. 1931. Prinzipien der historischen phonologie. *Travaux du cercle linguistique de Prague*, 4:246–267.

Shinae Kang and Clara Cohen. 2016. Relationships between functional load and auditory confusability under different speech environments. In *Interspeech 2016*. International Speech Communication Association.

William Labov, Sharon Ash, and Charles Boberg. 2006. *Atlas of North American English: Phonology and phonetics*. Mouton de Gruyter, Berlin.

Roger Levy. 2008. A noisy-channel model of rational human sentence comprehension under uncertain input. In *Proceedings of the conference on empirical methods in natural language processing*, pages 234–243. Association for Computational Linguistics.

Paul A. Luce and David B. Pisoni. 1998. Recognizing spoken words. *Ear and Hearing*, 19(1):1–36.

R. Duncan Luce. 1959. *Individual Choice Behavior: A Theoretical Analysis*. John Wiley and Sons.

V. Malthesius. 1931. Zum Problem der Belastungs- und Kombinationsfähigkeit der Phoneme. *Travaux du cercle linguistique de Prague*, 4:148–152.

Andre Martinet. 1952. Function, structure, and sound change. *Word*, 8:1–32.

George A. Miller and Patricia E. Nicely. 1955. An analysis of perceptual confusions among some English consonants. *The Journal of the Acoustical Society of America*, 27(2):338–352.

Dennis Norris and James M. McQueen. 2008. Shortlist B.: a Bayesian model of continuous speech recognition. *Psychological review*, 115(2):357.

John J. Ohala. 1993a. The phonetics of sound change. In Charles Jones, editor, *Historical linguistics: Problems and perspectives*, pages 237–278. Longman Publishing.

John J. Ohala. 1993b. Sound change as nature's speech perception experiment. *Speech Communication*, 13(1-2):155–161.

Dinoj Surendran and Partha Niyogi. 2003. Measuring the usefulness (functional load) of phonological contrasts. Technical report, Technical Report TR-2003.

Dinoj Surendran and Partha Niyogi. 2006. Quantifying the functional load of phonemic oppositions, distinctive features, and suprasegmentals. In O. N. Thomson, editor, *Competing models of linguistic change: Evolution and beyond*, pages 43–58. John Benjamins, Amsterdam.

Tsz-Him Tsui. 2012. Tonal variation in Hong Kong Cantonese acoustic distance & functional load. In *Proceedings from the Annual Meeting of the Chicago Linguistic Society*, volume 48, pages 579–588. Chicago Linguistic Society.

Marilyn D. Wang and Robert C. Bilger. 1973. Consonant confusions in noise: A study of perceptual features. *The Journal of the Acoustical Society of America*, 54(5):1248–1266.

Andrew Wedel, Abby Kaplan, and Scott Jackson. 2013. High functional load inhibits phonological contrast loss: A corpus study. *Cognition*, 128(2):179–186.

Robert L. Weide. 1998. The CMU pronouncing dictionary [cmudict 0.7].

"Oh, I've Heard That Before": Modelling Own-Dialect Bias After Perceptual Learning by Weighting Training Data

Rachael Tatman
Department of Linguistics
University of Washington
rctatman@uw.edu

Abstract

Human listeners are able to quickly and robustly adapt to new accents and do so by using information about speaker's identities. This paper will present experimental evidence that, even considering information about speaker's identities, listeners retain a strong bias towards the acoustics of their own dialect after dialect learning. Participants' behaviour was accurately mimicked by a classifier which was trained on more cases from the base dialect and fewer from the target dialect. This suggests that imbalanced training data may result in automatic speech recognition errors consistent with those of speakers from populations over-represented in the training data.

1 Introduction

Accent adaptation is an on-going challenge for automatic speech recognition (ASR) systems. However, a system does exist which adapts quickly and robustly to new accents: human speech perception, and in particular perceptual learning of new dialects.

This is a process which has been extensively researched in the fields of sociolinguistics and phonetics. It is well established that listeners do learn to perceive new language varieties (Fox, 1974; Hay et al., 2010; Sumner, 2011), and that they use world knowledge and their social beliefs about speakers to do so (Niedzielski, 1999; Johnson et al., 1999; Hay and Drager, 2010).

While modelling perceptual learning may lead to more human-like accent adaptation, to be a good cognitive model, it must capture behaviours found in experimental work: own-dialect bias, and the use of world knowledge during adaptation.

2 Experiment

2.1 Mainstream United States and New Zealand English

This experiment used acoustic data taken from sociologically-matched speakers of two distinct dialects: Mainstream US English (MUSE) and New Zealand English (NZE). The front vowels of MUSE and NZE vowels very confusable; due to an on-going vowel shift in NZE, the vowel in NZE "head" is very similar to the vowel in MUSE "hid", and NZE "had" sounds very like MUSE "head" (Watson, 2014). This overlap can be seen in Figure 3. Naive MUSE speakers listening to NZE, then, tend to make systematic errors when reporting which word they have heard. To evaluate this confusion, this experiment used a lexical identification task, where participants reported which word they believe a sound to be from.

2.2 Experimental Paradigm

First, listeners took a demographic questionnaire to ensure that they were from the United States, that they had not travelled to New Zealand and that they were unfamiliar with New Zealand English. Any listener not meeting these criteria was excluded from the experiment.

Listeners completed three lexical identification tasks. In each task, they were played a 300ms audio sample taken from the steady-state of the vowel from one of the words "heed", "head" or "had". Only the vowel was used in order to avoid possible confounds of variation in stop-production across dialects (Lyle, 2008). "Hid" tokens were excluded due to a very salient duration contrast in NZE between the vowel in "hid" and other vowels (Langstrof, 2009). Audio data was taken from two speakers of NZE and one speaker of MUSE. All speakers were white women between the ages of 20 and 30, with a college-level education or

Proceedings of the 7th Workshop on Cognitive Modeling and Computational Linguistics (CMCL 2017), pages 29–34,
Valencia, Spain, April 7, ©2017 Association for Computational Linguistics

higher.

The first lexical identification task was designed to train listeners to correctly identify the vowels of NZE. Listeners were played a vowel and asked to input which word it had come from: "heed", "head", "had" or "hid". If they picked the right word, they were told that it was correct and played a different token. If they picked the wrong one, they were told that they were incorrect, which word the token had been taken from and were given another chance to answer correctly. This process continued until each listener correctly labelled ten tokens in a row. For this task, listeners heard audio a single speaker of NZE and were told that the speaker was from New Zealand.

For the next two tasks, listeners did not receive feedback. In one task they were played audio from a MUSE speaker, and in the other from a second NZE speaker. They were explicitly told before each task the national origin of the speaker they were about to hear: New Zealand or the United States. However, while half of the listeners were given the correct information about each speaker, the other half were given incorrect information about each.

Twenty-one listeners participated in this experiment, most of whom (17) were from the West dialect region (Labov et al., 2005). The experiment was administered on-line using PsyToolkit (Stoet, 2010), and participants were recruited using social media and word of mouth.

3 Experimental Results

All participants were able to learn to successfully label the vowels of New Zealand English. This can be seen be seen in Figure 1: when given the correct social information about the speaker, the classifications of vowels from both MUSE and NZE were generally correct, with an average F_1 across classes of 0.96 and 0.75, respectively.

Being given incorrect information about a speaker's national origin, e.g. being told that a speaker from New Zealand was from the United States affected listeners classifications differently depending on the actual regional origin of the speaker. While listeners were still fairly accurate on their own dialect (F_1=0.81), the categorically changed their judgements for NZE (F_1=0.56). This difference can clearly be seen in Figure 2. The categorical changes are in line with confusions discussed in Section 2.1. NZE "head" is

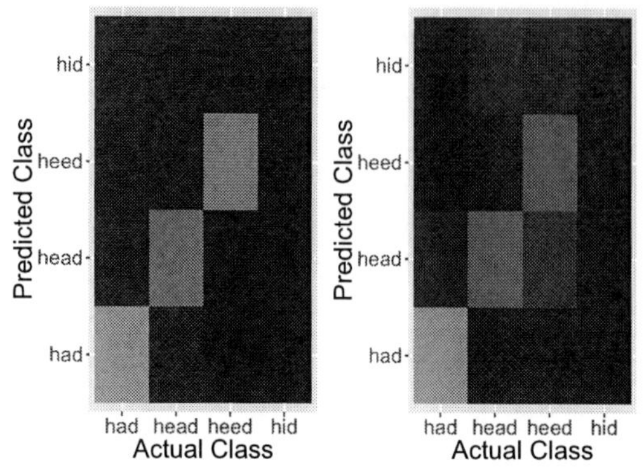

Figure 1: Heatmaps of the confusion matrix for MUSE (left) and NZE (right) classifications when participants were told the correct regional origin of the speaker. Note that, in both cases, most classifications were correct, i.e. on the center diagonal.

mis-classified as "hid", and NZE "had" is misclassified as "head".

In other words, when listeners from the United States are listening to a speaker from New Zealand that they have been told is also from the United States, they are classifying NZE vowels as if they were from MUSE. However, the inverse is not true. Even when told that a MUSE speaker is from New Zealand, listeners are still classifying their vowels as if they believed them to be from the United States. This preference for vowel classifications in line with those of a listener's own dialect will be referred to as "own-dialect bias" from this point on.

4 Computational Modelling

Based on the experimental data outlined above, any classifier of multi-dialect data should have the following qualities in order to achieve human-like classifications:

- Classifications should depend on information about the speaker's dialect.
- The classifier should should also consider one dialect the "default" and be biased towards it.

4.1 Data

To maximize parallelism, the same acoustic data was used to train classifiers as the participants were given. For each item, four features were recorded: the speaker's regional origin (NZ or

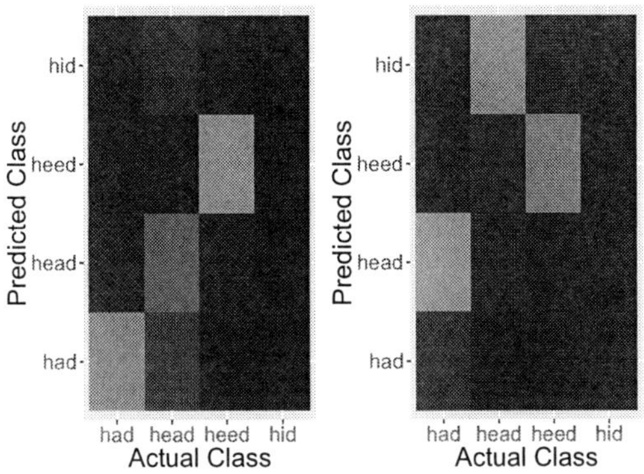

Figure 2: Heatmaps for the confusion matrix for MUSE (left) and NZE (right) classifications when participants were told the correct national origin of the speaker. While this had a slight effect on the classification of MUSE vowels, it categorically changed that of NZE vowels–this is what is meant by "own-dialect bias".

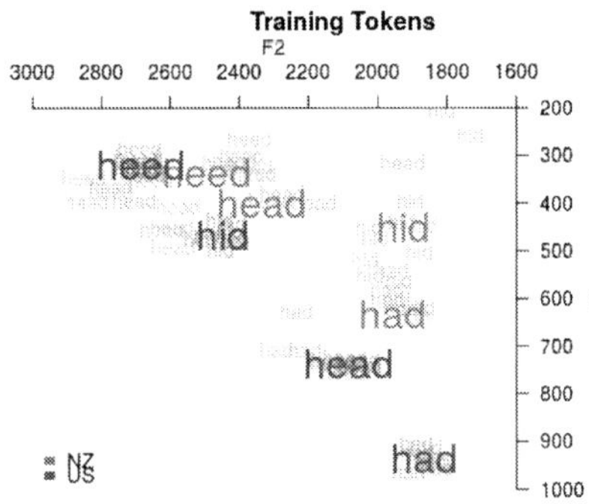

Figure 3: Plot of training tokens in a first by second formant space.

US), and the first, second and third formants as measured at the central point of the steady state of the vowel. Formants are frequency bands of high acoustic energy within the speech signal, and they are a robust cue to the identity of the vowel for human listeners (Wright, 2004). The vowels considered in this study are primarily distinguished by the first formant, as can be seen in Figure 3.

4.2 Conditional Inference Trees

Throughout this section, modelling is done using conditional inference trees (Hothorn et al., 2006). These are decision trees where nodes are split based on statistical inference rather than information gain. As a result, they are not biased towards factors with more levels, including numeric factors

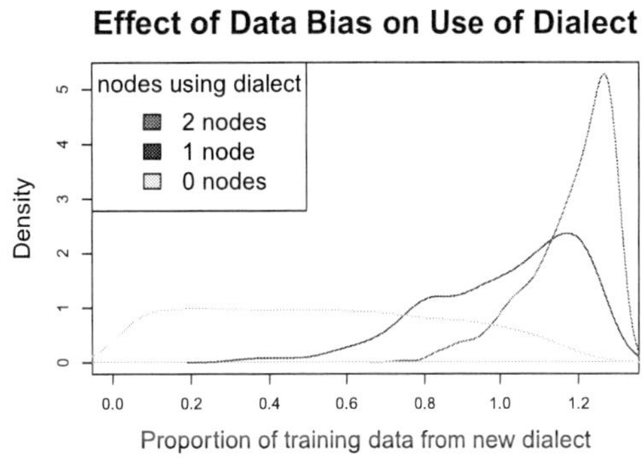

Figure 4: Figure showing how bias in training data affects the degree to which dialect information is used during classification. The more data from the second dialect is added to the original dialect, the more nodes in conditional inference tree will split based on dialect.

like formant values.

Another benefit of conditional inference trees is ease of interpretation. It is clear how each feature is being used during classification and to what extent it is affecting classifications, which allows a clear comparison between different conditional inference trees.

4.3 Bias as Exposure

One way to model own-dialect bias is to compare models trained on datasets where there is bias towards one dialect. To simulate this, 4500 conditional inference trees were trained. The proportion of NZE training tokens to MUSE token was varied between 0.02 (only 1 NZE token) to 1.3 (45 NZE tokens), with a uniform distribution. As the proportion of training tokens from the second dialect increased, so did the number of nodes in the conditional inference tree splitting based on speaker dialect. This can be seen in Figure 4.

A classifier trained on a dataset highly biased towards MUSE tokens was an excellent model of participants' own-dialect bias on mislabelled tokens from their own dialect. This can be seen in Figure 5. The classifications on the left are from a model trained on data strongly biased towards MUSE: 90% of the training data for this model came from MUSE. The classifications on the right are from a model trained on a dataset balanced between MUSE and NZE (50% each). The outputs of both models are based on MUSE data that has been mislabelled as being from NZE.

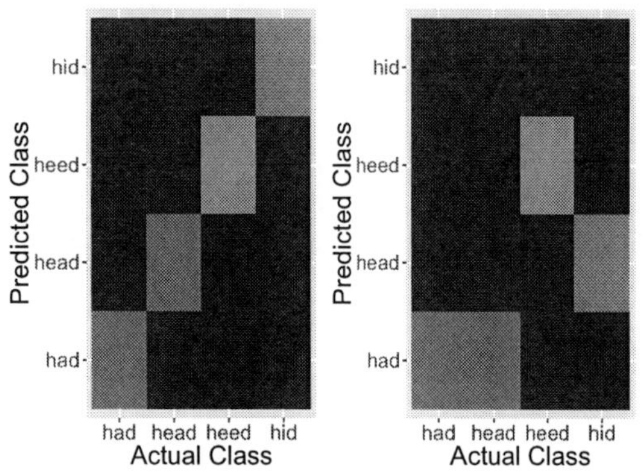

Figure 5: Classifications by conditional inference trees trained on data biased towards MUSE (on left) or balanced between MUSE and NZE (on right). These two classifiers are both showing classifications on MUSE tokens mislabelled as NZE. In this case, the biased classifier is a better behavioural model.

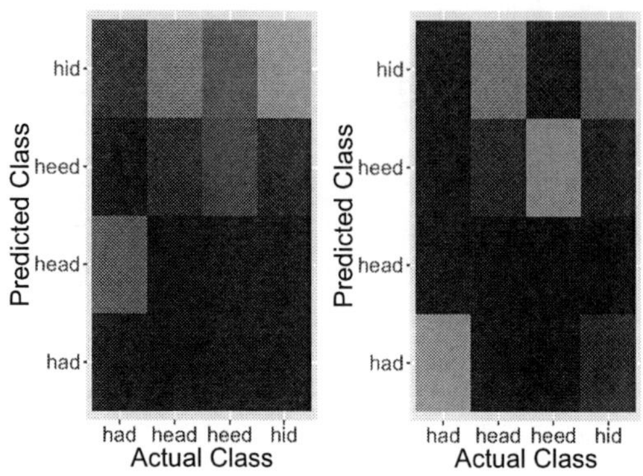

Figure 6: Classifications of NZE tokens mislabelled as MUSE by classifiers trained on data biased towards MUSE (left) or balanced between MUSE and NZE (right). While the balanced training data resulted in more accurate classifications, the biased model is a much more accurate behavioural model.

The biased model has classifications much more in line with human participants than the balanced one right. The overall accuracy of biased model (F_1=1.00) was also closer to that of human participants (F_1=0.97) than the accuracy of the unbiased model (F_1=0.85).

The model trained on biased data also proved a much better behavioural model for NZE data mislabelled as being MUSE. This can be seen in Figure 6. Again, the biased model is the on the left and the balanced on the right. In particular, the biased model shows the same confusion pattern as human participants, with "had" mislabelled as "head" and "head" mislabelled as "hid". While the model trained on balanced data is more accurate (F_1=0.74, as opposed to F_1=0.48 for the biased model), it is a much closer approximation of participant behaviour; participants were very poor at this task in terms of raw accuracy (F_1=0.56).

Conceptually, we can think of the addition of nodes splitting on dialect as modelling the fact that the more exposure a listener has to a dialect, the more likely they are to make distinctions between that dialect and their own. This is supported by research which shows that listeners are better at identifying dialects the more they have been exposed to them, which has been found in both English (Clopper and Pisoni, 2004; Baker et al., 2009) and Spanish (Díaz-Campos and Navarro-Galisteo, 2009).

4.4 Response time

While greater exposure to multiple dialects may improve comprehension accuracy overall, it does come at a cost. It has been previously found that lexical selection is slower for listeners who have been exposed to multiple dialects (Clopper and Walker, 2016). While all participants in this experiment were exposed to multiple dialects, we can compare their response times for "heed" (which was very similar across both dialects) to those for "had" and "head" tokens (which diverged). A one-way ANOVA of log-transformed response times in milliseconds found a significant effect of word ($F(2,4029)=20.63$, $p < 0.01$)). Response times for "heed" ($\mu = 1168.38, \sigma = 541.13$) were the fastest, followed by "had" ($\mu = 1196.62, \sigma = 510.59$) and "head" ($\mu = 1298.16, \sigma = 563.39$). So response times for tokens confusable across dialects was slower than for those tokens not those participants were exposed to less variability for. This can be seen in Figure 7.

This seems even more reasonable given that most conditional inference trees trained on this data, such as the one shown in Figure 8, require travelling through more nodes to classify of "hid", "head" or "head" than they do to classify "heed". Since making a decision at each node takes time, moving through fewer nodes would result in a faster response time.

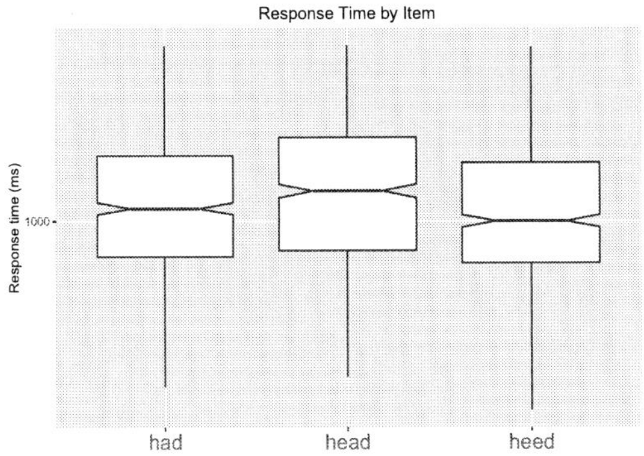

Figure 7: Response time, in milliseconds, by token type. Note that "heed" tokens, which were similar across dialects and thus didn't require dialect-specific learning, were categorized most quickly.

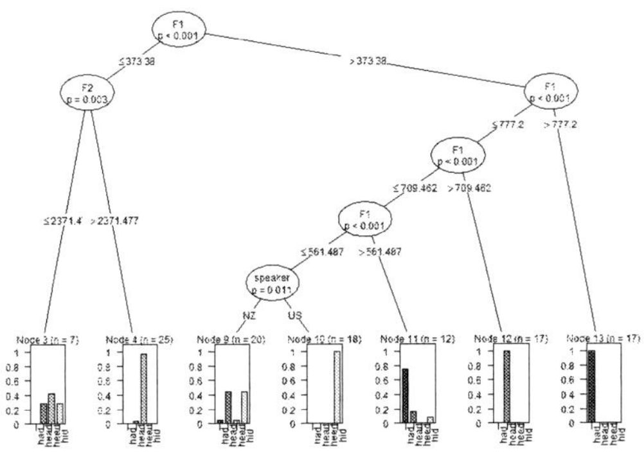

Figure 8: Conditional inference tree trained on balanced MUSE and NZE data. Note that all "heed" classifications occur in nodes 3 and 4 and require travelling through only two other nodes.

5 Discussion

This paper has provided experimental evidence that human listeners maintain a perceptual bias towards their own dialect even after successful perceptual learning. These findings are not surprising given previous findings of social bias towards ones own dialect (Coupland and Bishop, 2007; Floccia et al., 2006), as well as findings in the speech perception literature.

Early work on the perceptual magnet effect (Kuhl, 1991), for example, showed that listeners have a perceptual preference for vowels they are more familiar with, which was attributed to the location of prototypes. Later work on episodic learning casts this preference in terms of a higher density of exemplars in this area (Johnson, 1997; Pierrehumbert, 2001).

Though the modelling results discussed here do fit well with the larger claims of exemplar theory, they are not an explicit extension of it. Note that the balanced conditional inference tree model is not explicitly conditioned on the biased models; each is a separate, independent model. This differs from the Bayesian belief-updating modelling often employed in exemplar theory. Learning can be modelled in this framework in much the same way, however. Training a new model on a dataset that is a superset of the previous training set would allow for "updating" of the model.

The model presented here was weighted to show own-dialect bias. However, there is nothing to stop the weighting from going the other way, which would suggest that it's possible for a listener to be biased *away* from their own dialect. Given that this has previously been observed in phonetics research, this is a feature rather than a bug. With enough exposure to a second dialect, especially if their attitude towards the second dialect is positive, speaker's production and perception can both shift towards the new dialect (Evans and Iverson, 2007; Sumner and Samuel, 2009).

The effect of bias in training data on the classification of conditional inference tree models closely parallels human listener's biases towards their own dialect. While this is desirable from a behavioural modelling perspective, dialectically-biased training data also resulted in lower accuracy on the dialect it was biased against. This suggests that systems trained primarily on one dialect should make the same types of errors on other dialects as a speaker of the training dialect would. In this case, an ASR system trained on MUSE data would make systematic errors on NZE.

This model also provides an alternate way to include speaker dialect during automatic speech recognition. Rather than training separate models on each dialect (Telaar and Fuhs, 2013; Najafian et al., 2014), dialect can be included within decision-tree based acoustic models (Young et al., 1994). This may be especially helpful for closely related dialects or varieties that share phones. It may, however, come with a cost. Given the response time data discussed in Section 4.4, an accurate behavioural model capable of multi-dialect recognition would respond more slowly to tokens that are confusable between the dialects it was trained on.

References

Wendy Baker, David Eddington, and Lyndsey Nay. 2009. Dialect identification: The effects of region of origin and amount of experience. *American Speech*, 84(1):48–71.

Cynthia G. Clopper and David B. Pisoni. 2004. Homebodies and army brats: Some effects of early linguistic experience and residential history on dialect categorization. *Language Variation and Change*, 16(01):31–48.

Cynthia G. Clopper and Abby Walker. 2016. Effects of lexical competition and dialect exposure on phonological priming. *Language and Speech*, page 0023830916643737.

Nikolas Coupland and Hywel Bishop. 2007. Ideologised values for British accents. *Journal of sociolinguistics*, 11(1):74–93.

Manuel Díaz-Campos and Inmaculada Navarro-Galisteo. 2009. Perceptual categorization of dialect variation in spanish. In *Selected Proceedings of the 11th Hispanic Linguistics Symposium*, pages 179–195.

Bronwen G. Evans and Paul Iverson. 2007. Plasticity in vowel perception and production: A study of accent change in young adults. *The Journal of the Acoustical Society of America*, 121(6):3814–3826.

Caroline Floccia, Jeremy Goslin, Frédérique Girard, and Gabrielle Konopczynski. 2006. Does a regional accent perturb speech processing? *Journal of Experimental Psychology: Human Perception and Performance*, 32(5):1276.

Robert Allen Fox. 1974. An experiment in cross-dialect vowel perception. In *Tenth Regional Meeting–Chicago Linguistic Society*, pages 178–185.

Jennifer Hay and Katie Drager. 2010. Stuffed toys and speech perception. *Linguistics*, 48(4):865–892.

Jen Hay, Katie Drager, and Paul Warren. 2010. Short-term exposure to one dialect affects processing of another. *Language and speech*, 53(4):447–471.

Torsten Hothorn, Kurt Hornik, and Achim Zeileis. 2006. Unbiased recursive partitioning: A conditional inference framework. *Journal of Computational and Graphical statistics*, 15(3):651–674.

Keith Johnson, Elizabeth A. Strand, and Mariapaola D'Imperio. 1999. Auditory–visual integration of talker gender in vowel perception. *Journal of Phonetics*, 27(4):359–384.

Keith Johnson. 1997. Speech perception without speaker normalization: An exemplar model. *Talker variability in speech processing*, pages 145–165.

Patricia K. Kuhl. 1991. Human adults and human infants show a perceptual magnet effect for the prototypes of speech categories, monkeys do not. *Attention, Perception, & Psychophysics*, 50(2):93–107.

William Labov, Sharon Ash, and Charles Boberg. 2005. *The atlas of North American English: Phonetics, phonology and sound change*. Walter de Gruyter.

Christian Langstrof. 2009. On the role of vowel duration in the New Zealand English front vowel shift. *Language Variation and Change*, 21(3):437.

Samantha Lyle. 2008. *Dialect variation in stop consonant voicing*. Ph.D. thesis, The Ohio State University.

Maryam Najafian, Saeid Safavi, Abualsoud Hanani, and Martin Russell. 2014. Acoustic model selection using limited data for accent robust speech recognition. In *Signal Processing Conference (EUSIPCO), 2014 Proceedings of the 22nd European*, pages 1786–1790. IEEE.

Nancy Niedzielski. 1999. The effect of social information on the perception of sociolinguistic variables. *Journal of language and social psychology*, 18(1):62–85.

Janet Pierrehumbert. 2001. lenition and contrast. *Frequency and the emergence of linguistic structure*, 45:137.

Gijsbert Stoet. 2010. Psytoolkit: A software package for programming psychological experiments using linux. *Behavior Research Methods*, 42(4):1096–1104.

Meghan Sumner and Arthur G. Samuel. 2009. The effect of experience on the perception and representation of dialect variants. *Journal of Memory and Language*, 60(4):487–501.

Meghan Sumner. 2011. The role of variation in the perception of accented speech. *Cognition*, 119(1):131–136.

Dominic Telaar and Mark C. Fuhs. 2013. Accent- and speaker-specific polyphone decision trees for non-native speech recognition. In *INTERSPEECH*, pages 3313–3316.

Catherine Watson. 2014. Mappings between vocal tract area functions, vocal tract resonances and speech formants for multiple speakers. In *Fifteenth Annual Conference of the International Speech Communication Association*.

Richard Wright. 2004. A review of perceptual cues and cue robustness. *Phonetically based phonology*, pages 34–57.

Steve J. Young, Julian J. Odell, and Philip C. Woodland. 1994. Tree-based state tying for high accuracy acoustic modelling. In *Proceedings of the workshop on Human Language Technology*, pages 307–312. Association for Computational Linguistics.

Inherent Biases of Recurrent Neural Networks for Phonological Assimilation and Dissimilation

Amanda Doucette
University of Massachusetts Amherst
amandakdoucette@gmail.com

Abstract

A recurrent neural network model of phonological pattern learning is proposed. The model is a relatively simple neural network with one recurrent layer, and displays biases in learning that mimic observed biases in human learning. Single-feature patterns are learned faster than two-feature patterns, and vowel or consonant-only patterns are learned faster than patterns involving vowels and consonants, mimicking the results of laboratory learning experiments. In non-recurrent models, capturing these biases requires the use of alpha features or some other representation of repeated features, but with a recurrent neural network, these elaborations are not necessary.

1 Introduction

Models of phonological pattern learning typically require large numbers of constraints or rules on where features can occur, and the presence of alpha features or some other representation of repeated features to allow certain patterns to be learned more quickly (Hayes and Wilson, 2008; Moreton et al., 2015). In human learning experiments, certain phonological patterns are learned more easily, particularly those involving multiple occurences of the same feature, such as a voicing agreement pattern.

In order to capture this bias towards single-feature patterns, many models have some representation of repeated features. Alpha features are one example of this (see McCarthy (1988) for other approaches, such as feature geometry). Alpha features allow a model to learn a harmony pattern with only one predicate - that two features must be the same, having the value α. Without alpha features, the model must learn two predicates - that the two features must either both have the value $+$ or the value $-$. Therefore, there cannot be a bias towards single-feature patterns, because two-feature patterns also require learning two predicates (Moreton, 2012).

In addition to alpha features, many phonological learning models have to test or search over a large number of possible rules or constraints to learn a pattern. In models that use conjunctions of features as constraints (Hayes and Wilson, 2008; Moreton et al., 2015), if there are N features in the model, each with three possible values ($+, -, \pm$), there are 3^N possible conjunctions of these features. With even a small number of features, the number of conjunctive constraints becomes very large.

Moreton, Pater, and Pertsova (2015) describe a cue-based learning model that uses these conjunctive constraints. Their model is a maximum entropy model trained by gradient descent on negative log-likelihood, and is related to the single-layer perceptron. It successfully models the biases found in human phonological learning experiments, but still requires listing all possible constraint conjuncions in the input. In unpublished work, I have found that it is also possible to model these biases without constraint conjunctions using a feed-forward neural network with a hidden layer. See Alderete and Tupper (To appear) for an overview of other connectionist approaches to phonology.

Hare (1990) uses a recurrent neural network to model Hungarian vowel harmony without phonological rules or constraints. In Hare's model, sequences of individual features describing vowels were the only inputs to the network. Some features in the input sequence could be left unspecified, and after training, fully specified feature sequences are output. While the model was only

Proceedings of the 7th Workshop on Cognitive Modeling and Computational Linguistics (CMCL 2017), pages 35–40,
Valencia, Spain, April 7, ©2017 Association for Computational Linguistics

trained on sequences of vowels, not entire words, Hare showed that recurrent neural networks were capable of modeling vowel harmony patterns using only individual features as input.

Rodd (1997) also uses recurrent neural networks to model Turkish vowel harmony. Individual phonemes rather than features were used as input to the networks, and the task was to predict the following phoneme. Rodd showed that the hidden units in small recurrent networks were able to represent distinctions between vowels and consonants, differences in sonority, and differences between front and back vowels. Although humans most likely do not perform the task of predicting the next phoneme in a word, Rodd showed that simple recurrent network could learn phonological regularities through differences in the distribution of phonemes.

Recurrent neural networks are capable of learning more than just vowel harmony patterns and feature representations, though. This paper describes a simple recurrent neural network model of phonological pattern learning that is biased towards learning single-feature patterns and patterns over only consonants or vowels without using alpha features, separate representations of consonants and vowels, or conjunctive constraints.

2 Model

The model used in these simulations is a simple recurrent neural network model. The "words" that make up the patterns are the inputs in the first layer of the model. At each time step, the four features representing one phoneme are input to the network. The second layer is a hidden recurrent layer with ten neurons. The third layer is a log softmax layer with two output neurons. After the entire sequence is input to the model, the outputs at the final timestep will represent the log probabilities of the input belonging to each of the two classes, which will be referred to as IN the pattern or OUT of the pattern. The probability of a pattern being IN or OUT is the probability of it being allowed in the language.

The model was trained using gradient descent on negative log-likelihood with a learning rate of 0.01. Weights were adjusted after each word in the training data, rather than in batches. In each epoch of training, the order of presentation of the training data was randomly permuted. The output of the network was considered to be correct when the log probability of the intended class was greater than the other class. This criterion for correctness was used because when the model is trained on a subset of the full pattern, it prevents overfitting to that subset. After each epoch of training, all training examples were checked for correctness. If the correct class was predicted for every training example, training was stopped.

The number of neurons in the recurrent layer is not important to the model. Ten neurons were chosen because with fewer neurons, the patterns tested could not be fully learned, and with more, the patterns were learned after only a few training epochs. More complex patterns or patterns requiring more features will likely require a larger number of neurons in this layer.

3 Patterns

The patterns used in testing the model used four phonological features - two consonant features, and two vowel features. Each feature has a value of +1 or -1. For consonants, the vowel features have a value of 0, and for vowels, the consonants have a value of 0. The consonant features used in these patterns are voicing ($+/-$voi) and place($+/-$cor), and the vowel features are height ($+/-$hi) and backness ($+/-$back). This feature set corresponds to the consonants [d, t, k, g] and the vowels [i, u, æ, a]. All "words" in the patterns have the form $C_1V_1C_2V_2$, where C and V range over the four consonants and vowels described by the four features, so there are 256 total. For each pattern, the words are divided into the two classes, IN and OUT, each with 128 examples.

Six patterns, dividing the 256 words based on their features, were created as simplified versions of real phonological patterns. The six feature combinations that are IN for each pattern are described in Table 1. The 128 words that do not fit these feature descriptions are in the OUT class of the pattern.

In pattern 1, there is a feature dependency between an adjacent consonant and vowel. In pattern 2, this dependency is between a non-adjacent consonant and vowel. Pattern 3 is a voice assimilation pattern where the two consonants must agree in voicing. In pattern 4, the consonants must disagree in voicing. In pattern 5, the two features relevant to the pattern are on the same consonant, and in pattern 6, they are on two separate consonants.

Moreton (2012) claims that there is an advan-

Pattern	Features in Pattern
1	C1+voi and V1+back C1-voi and V1-back
2	C1+voi and V2+back C1-voi and V2-back
3	C1+voi and C2+voi C1-voi and C2-voi
4	C1+voi and C2-voi C1-voi and C2+voi
5	C1+voi and C1+cor C1-voi and C1-cor
6	C1+voi and C2+cor C1-voi and C2-cor

Table 1: Feature descriptions of patterns.

tage for learning intra-dimensional patterns over inter-dimensional patterns that requires alpha features to be captured by a model. The same advantage was also shown by Moreton, Pater, and Pertsova (2015) and Saffran and Thiessen (2003). In the six patterns described here, patterns 3 and 4 are intra-dimentional, single-feature patterns, and the rest are inter-dimensional, two-feature patterns. Therefore, patterns 3 and 4 should be learned faster than patterns 1, 2, and 6.

Pattern 5 is also an inter-dimensional pattern, but the two features are on the same segment rather than different segments like the rest of the patterns. In the experiments of Moreton, Pater, and Pertsova (2015), patterns involving features on the same segment were easier to learn than patterns involving two segments. Because of this, pattern 5 should be learned faster than pattern 6.

Moreton (2012) also showed in an experiment that a pattern involving an adjacent consonant and vowel was learned no faster than a pattern involving a non-adjacent consonant and vowel. Therefore, there should be no difference in the amount of time to learn patterns 1 and 2.

Results from several studies also show that there is no difference in difficulty of learning harmony and disharmony patterns (Moreton, 2012; Pycha et al., 2003; Skoruppa and Peperkamp, 2011). Of these six patterns, pattern 3 is a harmony pattern, and pattern 4 is a disharmony pattern, so there should be no difference in the time to learn these patterns.

4 Results: Training on full patterns

For each pattern, the model was trained 3000 times with random initial weights on all 256 examples. For each training run, the number of epochs taken to learn the pattern according to the criterion in section 2 was recorded. Table 2 shows averages over the 3000 runs for each pattern. The model was capable of learning the patterns in all but 25 training runs, which were stopped after 400 epochs and excluded from these results. This was done because weights in these training runs were likely stuck in local minima, and the model was incapable of learning the pattern.

Pattern	Mean	St. Err.	St. Dev.
1	22.03	0.22	11.78
2	22.74	0.26	14.49
3	19.91	0.29	15.88
4	20.20	0.29	16.08
5	19.65	0.15	8.42
6	22.46	0.23	12.79

Table 2: Number of epochs to learn patterns with full training set.

In a two sample t-test, there is no evidence that there is a significant difference between the number of epochs taken to learn patterns 3 and 4, the harmony and disharmony patterns ($p > 0.01$). Patterns 3 and 4, the one-feature patterns, were learned significantly faster than patterns 1, 2, and 6, the two-feature patterns involving two segments in two sample t-tests ($p < 0.01$). However, there was no difference between the one-feature patterns 3 and 4, and pattern 5, which involved two features on the same segment ($p > 0.01$). Pattern 5 was also learned faster than pattern 6, which involved two features on different consonants ($p < 0.01$). There was also no difference between pattern 2, which involved a non-adjacent consonant and vowel, and pattern 1, which involved an adjacent consonant and vowel ($p > 0.01$). Individual comparisons and exact p-values are shown in Table 3.

5 Results: Training on subset of patterns

The model was also trained on randomly chosen subsets of the training data for each pattern. This was done because when learning phonological patterns, people do not have access to every possible example of the pattern, and every possible example of something that does not conform

Comparison	p-value
Pattern 1, Pattern 2	0.03934
Pattern 5, Pattern 6	2.2×10^{-16}
Pattern 1, Pattern 3	4.091×10^{-9}
Pattern 2, Pattern 3	6.505×10^{-13}
Pattern 4, Pattern 3	0.4843
Pattern 5, Pattern 3	0.4361
Pattern 6, Pattern 3	8.932×10^{-12}
Pattern 1, Pattern 4	4.583×10^{-7}
Pattern 2, Pattern 4	1.414×10^{-10}
Pattern 5, Pattern 4	0.1006
Pattern 6, Pattern 4	1.909×10^{-9}

Table 3: Training time comparisons for pairs of patterns and p-values.

to the pattern. Rather, people are only exposed to correct examples of their language as they learn.

To test the model under these conditions, 32 examples of each pattern were randomly chosen from the 128 available. If the model were trained on only positive examples, it would predict everything to be included in the pattern, so some negative training examples are needed. As negative training examples, 32 were chosen from the remaining 224, after removing the 32 already selected positive examples. Therefore, the negative examples are not true negative examples, they are just randomly chosen examples from the full dataset.

Although this is an unusual method of training a neural network model, it was done to test if the model is capable of generalizing to unseen examples of the pattern. There is no direct way of using unsupervised learning with a recurrent neural network, so using randomly selected negative examples was used as an analogue to it. In training, the model gets positive examples of the pattern, but does not get true negative examples.

The model was trained 3000 times on randomly chosen subsets of each pattern. Training was stopped when the model correctly classified the 64 examples it was trained on. After each training run, the proportion of the full dataset that was classified correctly by the model was recorded. Table 3 shows averages over the 3000 runs for the number of training epochs taken and proportion correct in the full dataset for each pattern. 41 training runs were excluded because the pattern was not learned in 400 epochs.

When trained on a subset of the pattern, the

Patt.	Mean Corr.	Mean	Std. Err.	Std. Dev.
1	0.73	125.6	0.67	36.6
2	0.64	131.1	0.69	37.6
3	0.72	133.8	0.77	42.3
4	0.72	130.8	0.72	39.3
5	0.76	125.7	0.72	39.6
6	0.69	125.0	0.66	36.0

Table 4: Number of epochs to learn patterns with partial training set.

mean number of epochs taken to learn each pattern did not differ in the way they did when trained on the entire pattern. The mean number of epochs taken is similar for each pattern, with a much larger standard deviation than when the model was trained on the full pattern. This is likely because the subsets were randomly chosen. Sometimes the negative examples in the subset would conflict with the pattern represented by the positive examples, resulting in much longer training times.

While the training times do not follow the predicted pattern, these results show that the model is still able to generalize the pattern to examples it is not trained on, as shown in the mean proportion correct column in Table 3. The model was trained on 25% of the pattern data, only 12.5% of which were positive examples of the pattern, but can correctly classify 64% to 76% of the examples.

6 Discussion and conclusion

Without a representation of repeated features, and using only single features as input, this recurrent neural network is able to model results from human phonological learning experiments. Although non-recurrent neural network models such as the single-layer perceptron require a representation of repeated features to allow single-feature patterns to be learned more easily (Moreton, 2012), the addition of a recurrent layer seems to have the same effect. In a recurrent neural network, input is processed one segment at a time, rather than simultaneously. There is no clear way to represent sequential input in non-recurrent models. Although it is difficult to interpret connection weights in a recurrent neural network, it is possible that the sequential input of the network somehow biases it towards single-feature patterns.

A non-recurrent, multilayer perceptron may be able to learn these patterns because they are all the same length, but it will not be able to capture the bias towards patterns with repeated features. By concatenating the features of all four segments into one input to a multilayer perceptron, there is no connection between segments with repeated features; a pattern involving two instances of a consonant feature will be connected to the hidden layer in the same way a pattern with a consonant and a vowel will be. In a recurrent network, repeated activation of the same input feature will increase activation in a hidden unit more than activation of different features in the input will. For this reason, a non-recurrent network cannot model biases towards single-feature patterns.

In addition to the bias towards single-feature patterns, the recurrent neural network can learn patterns over only consonants or only vowels more quickly than patterns involving a consonant and a vowel. Some models accomplish this with an additional representation of only the vowels in a word, or only the consonants in a vowel or consonant 'tier' (Hayes and Wilson, 2008). A vowel tier allows for a bias towards vowel-only patterns because only the vowels in a word are considered, making finding the pattern much faster.

This recurrent neural network model does not have any representation of a consonant or vowel tier, but it is still able to learn consonant-only patterns faster. There are separate features used for describing vowels and consonants, but they are all used as input to the network at the same time. This bias is possibly related to the single-feature bias. Vowels and consonants never have the same features, so patterns with only consonants or vowels are learned faster because there is some overlap in the features used to describe them. It is possible that adding a separate representation of vowels and consonants could make learning these patterns faster, but it does not seem necessary. However, this could be accomplished by having multiple instances of the model where only consonants, only vowels, or the entire word is input. The outputs of the recurrent layers of these separate instances would be connected to a single non-recurrent layer which would combine the predictions of the three tiers.

Although the patterns used to test the model can be described with only one or two features, it should also be capable of learning more complex patterns. More neurons in the input and recurrent layers will allow more input features to be used, and more complex patterns to be represented.

The model also requires supervised training. To learn a pattern, both positive and negative examples are necessary for the model, but humans are capable of learning these patterns through unsupervised learning (Moreton et al., 2015). Unsupervised learning can be approximated by using randomly chosen examples from the entire dataset as negative examples, but it is still not true unsupervised learning. If there is a way to better approximate unsupervised learning with this model, it would better fit the human learning experiments.

In conclusion, a simple recurrent neural network was able to model human phonological pattern learning without alpha features or any representation of rules or constraints. The model uses only individual phonological features as input, and has no separate representations of vowels or consonants. Single-feature patterns are learned more easily than two-feature patterns, and vowel or consonant-only patterns are learned more easily than patterns involving vowels and consonants. Modeling these biases using a recurrent neural network is possible without any representation of repeated features that is necessary in non-recurrent models.

Acknowledgments

Thanks to Joe Pater and Brendan O'Connor for their guidance and helpful discussion while I worked on this research, as well as to the four anonymous reviewers for their comments.

References

John Alderete and Paul Tupper. To appear. Connectionist approaches to generative phonology. In Anna Bosch and S. J. Hannahs, editors, *The Routledge handbook of phonological theory*.

Mary Hare. 1990. The role of trigger-target similarity in the vowel harmony process. In *Annual Meeting of the Berkeley Linguistics Society*, volume 16, pages 140–152.

Bruce Hayes and Colin Wilson. 2008. A maximum entropy model of phonotactics and phonotactic learning. *Linguistic Inquiry*, 39(3):379–440.

John J. McCarthy. 1988. Feature geometry and dependency: A. review. *Phonetica*, 45(2-4):84–108.

Elliott Moreton, Joe Pater, and Katya Pertsova. 2015. Phonological concept learning. *Cognitive Science*.

Elliott Moreton. 2012. Inter-and intra-dimensional dependencies in implicit phonotactic learning. *Journal of Memory and Language*, 67(1):165–183.

Anne Pycha, Pawel Nowak, Eurie Shin, and Ryan Shosted. 2003. Phonological rule-learning and its implications for a theory of vowel harmony. In *Proceedings of the 22nd West Coast Conference on Formal Linguistics*, volume 22, pages 101–114. Somerville, MA: Cascadilla Press.

Jennifer M. Rodd. 1997. Recurrent neural-network learning of phonological regularities in Turkish. In *CoNLL*, pages 97–106.

Jenny R. Saffran and Erik D. Thiessen. 2003. Pattern induction by infant language learners. *Developmental Psychology*, 39(3):484.

Katrin Skoruppa and Sharon Peperkamp. 2011. Adaptation to novel accents: Feature-based learning of context-sensitive phonological regularities. *Cognitive Science*, 35(2):348–366.

Predicting Japanese scrambling in the wild

Naho Orita
Graduate School of Information Sciences
Tohoku University
naho@ecei.tohoku.ac.jp

Abstract

Japanese speakers have a choice between canonical SOV and scrambled OSV word order to express the same meaning. Although previous experiments examine the influence of one or two factors for scrambling in a controlled setting, it is not yet known what kinds of multiple effects contribute to scrambling. This study uses naturally distributed data to test the multiple effects on scrambling simultaneously. A regression analysis replicates the NP length effect and suggests the influence of noun types, but it provides no evidence for syntactic priming, given-new ordering, and the animacy effect. These findings only show evidence for sentence-internal factors, but we find no evidence that discourse level factors play a role.

1 Introduction

Speakers constantly make choices about the form of their utterances such as referring expressions (Givón, 1983; Ariel, 1990; Gundel et al., 1993) and word order (Bock and Irwin, 1980; Arnold et al., 2000; Birner and Ward, 2009). For example, Japanese speakers have a choice between canonical SOV and scrambled OSV to convey the same meaning of the sentence as in (1).

(1) a. Taro-ga inu-o oikaketa.
Taro-NOM dog-ACC chased
'Taro chased the dog.'

b. Inu-o Taro-ga oikaketa.
dog-ACC Taro-NOM chased
'Taro chased the dog.'

The positioning of the direct object in (1b), scrambling (Saito, 1985; Saito and Hoji, 1983; Miyagawa, 1997), is known to be sensitive to such factors as length of the noun phrase (Yamashita and Chang, 2001), structural priming (Yamashita et al., 2002), given-new ordering of discourse participants (Ferreira and Yoshita, 2003), and animacy (Tanaka et al., 2011).

These experiments in language production examine the influence of one or two factors in a controlled experimental setting with a set of homogeneous stimuli that typically occur infrequently in the real world. However, as intensively discussed in Jaeger (2010), speakers' choices of sentence structure rather depend on the presence and interaction of multiple factors that are influenced by the probability distribution of preceding inputs.

This study complements previous psycholinguistic experiments in Japanese scrambling. We use a more representative set of Japanese sentences than those used in previous language production experiments and simultaneously test multiple effects on scrambling using a single regression analysis. This effort constitutes an initial step toward understanding Japanese scrambling in the wild that goes beyond laboratory data. The analysis replicates the effect of noun phrase length and suggests the influence of noun types, but it provides no evidence for syntactic priming, given-new ordering, and the animacy effect.

2 Related Work

2.1 Language production experiments

Although a body of research concerns the comprehension of scrambled sentences in Japanese (Koizumi and Tamaoka, 2010; Koizumi and Imamura, 2016, among many), the production counterpart has not been investigated to the same extent. Previous findings suggest that (i) Japanese speakers tend to put a longer object before a short subject via scrambling (Yamashita and Chang, 2001), (ii)

Proceedings of the 7th Workshop on Cognitive Modeling and Computational Linguistics (CMCL 2017), pages 41–45,
Valencia, Spain, April 7, ©2017 Association for Computational Linguistics

tend to produce the same structure as the prime sentence (Yamashita et al., 2002), (iii) are more likely to position animate entities earlier in the sentence than inanimate entities independent of their grammatical role and assign the subject role to animate entities (Tanaka et al., 2011), and (iv) tend to produce given arguments before new, where this effect is stronger when the previous mention of the given argument is lexically identical (Ferreira and Yoshita, 2003).

These experiments examine one or two hypotheses in a controlled setting to capture a precise mechanism of language production. However, it remains unknown whether and to what extent multiple effects contribute to observable behavior. This study complements these works by simultaneously testing multiple effects with naturally distributed data.

2.2 Corpus studies

Corpus studies examine the effect of some of the factors suggested above with more natural linguistic data. In Yamashita (2002), 19 scrambled sentences are found out of 2,635 sentences in Japanese magazines. Of these 19 scrambled sentences, 14 involve scrambling of "heavy" constituents that contain relative or subordinate clauses and 5 sentences contain anaphoric expressions that refer to preceding entities.

Imamura (2016) measures salience and information decay to investigate the distribution of subjects and objects in both SOV and OSV. He counts how many sentences stand between the argument and its referent to measure salience of the referent and how many times the argument is referred to after the target sentence to measure information decay. Analysis of 100 sentences for each word order that are randomly extracted from contemporary written Japanese texts (Maekawa et al., 2014) shows that the referent of the scrambled object tends to occur close to the scrambled sentence (i.e., old information), but is mentioned less frequently than the subject in successive sentences (i.e., not topical).

Although they explore more natural data than previous production experiments, they do not analyze the influence of multiple factors. Crucially, the sample size also is either limited (19 scrambled sentences in Yamashita (2002)) or intentionally balanced (100 sentences for each word order in Imamura (2016)). Moreover, they hand-code relevant information. These shortcomings make the analysis harder to extend to the wider data.

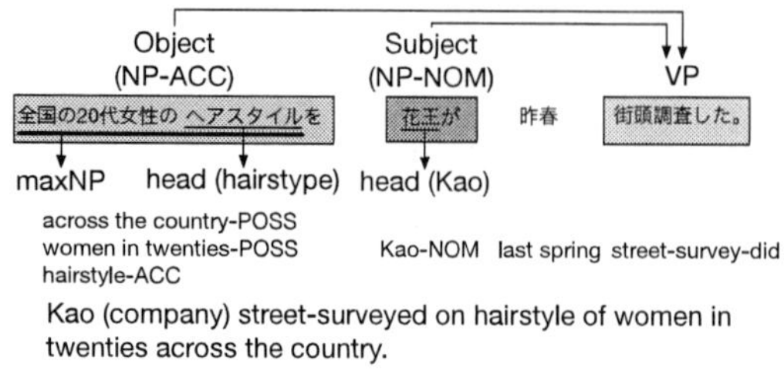

Figure 1: Illustration of the scrambled sentence extracted from the corpus

This study scales up these corpus studies by exploiting existing corpus annotations and by using a regression model that simultaneously tests multiple factors while handing unbalanced data. The following section describes the corpus and predictors in the analysis.

3 Predicting scrambling in Japanese

3.1 Corpus

We use NAIST Text Corpus (Iida et al., 2007) containing 2,929 documents (38,384 sentences) from Japanese newspapers. The corpus includes annotations of predicate-argument structure, event nouns, and coreferences along with morphological and syntactic information.

We use annotated dependency relations between arguments and the predicate to extract scrambled and canonical word order sentences. We extract pairs of nominative (NP with case marker *-ga*) and accusative (NP with case marker *-o*) arguments that depend on the same predicate (active voice only) as illustrated in Figure 1. We then check the linear order of these arguments. The result is 185 scrambled sentences and 2,918 canonical word order sentences. We exclude null arguments, which occur frequently in Japanese. The relatively small number of extracted sentences is primarily attributable to this exclusion.

3.2 Predictors

Based on previous findings as in Section 2, we extract the following information from the corpus and include it in the analysis.

Syntactic priming: We approximate the syntactic priming effect (Yamashita et al., 2002) using equation (1). It decays exponentially with the distance between the target sentence s_i and the

Predictor		$\hat{\beta}$	SE ($\hat{\beta}$)	z	p	$\chi^2(df)$	p_χ
SYNTACTIC PRIMING		0.67	0.57	1.16	0.24	1.23 (1)	0.27
SUBJECT GIVEN-NEW		-0.12	0.22	-0.53	0.60	0.28 (1)	0.60
OBJECT GIVEN-NEW		0.15	0.22	0.69	0.49	0.47 (1)	0.49
SUBJECT LENGTH		-0.15	0.02	-6.51	7.76e-11	65.28 (1)	6.49e-16
OBJECT LENGTH		0.12	0.01	10.59	<2e-16	107.71 (1)	3.11e-25
SUBJECT NOUNTYPE	NAME	-0.69	0.21	-3.26	0.001	16.70 (3)	<0.001
	VERBAL	-1.19	0.53	-2.26	0.02		
	FORMAL	-0.48	0.90	-0.54	0.59		
OBJECT NOUNTYPE	NAME	0.13	0.53	0.25	0.81	97.35 (3)	5.77e-21
	VERBAL	-0.36	0.20	-1.83	0.07		
	FORMAL	3.36	0.34	9.80	2e-16		

Table 1: Logistic model predicting scrambling for each sentence

scrambled sentence s_j as previously mentioned. If there is no scrambled sentence in the preceding discourse, we use parameter α that represents how likely speakers produce a scrambled sentence. We set this value at 0.01 in the analysis.

$$f(d_{i,j}) = \begin{cases} e^{-d_{i,j}/a} & \text{if } s_j \text{ exists} \\ \alpha & \text{if no } s_j \end{cases} \quad (1)$$

Given-new ordering: We measure the effect of given-new ordering, in particular, the effect of lexically identical mentions (Ferreira and Yoshita, 2003) by using the same function in (1). If there is a lexically identical word in the preceding discourse, we compute the distance between the target sentence s_i and the sentence containing the lexically identical word. We check all content words in the maxNP (a maximally spanning noun phrase as in Figure 1) and use the closest previous mention for computation. This is not a precise representation of given-new ordering in that we do not use coreference relations in contrast to Imamura (2016) that hand-annotated coreferences including bridging references.[1]

Length: The length of subject and object maxNPs in letters are included because the length has been shown to affect scrambling in Japanese (Yamashita and Chang, 2001; Yamashita, 2002).

Noun type: Scrambling is also correlated with animacy (Tanaka et al., 2011). There is no available animacy annotation in Japanese, but nouns in the NAIST Text Corpus are annotated with the type of information, such as proper names, verbal nouns, and formal nouns. Verbal nouns such as *kettei* 'decision' and *suisen* 'recommendation' can be verbs with the addition of a light verb *-suru* 'do'. Formal nouns such as *-koto* and *-mono* are a kind of nominalizer that lacks semantic content. Some formal nouns such as *-koto* and *-no* often function as a complementizer that takes a clausal complement (Inoue, 1976). We include these noun types in the analysis to capture automatically a coarse distinction between animate nouns and event/clausal expressions. Only the types of head nouns (illustrated in Figure 1) are included in the analysis. Other noun types such as common nouns (e.g., 'cat' and 'society') and temporal nouns (e.g., 'tomorrow') are excluded, but they account for the majority of the nouns in the corpus (about 65%).

4 Results

We use a logistic regression model wherein the outcome variable is the word order —i.e., scrambled or canonical. We include all predictors described above. The model was fitted using `glm` in R. Table 1 summarizes coefficient estimates $\hat{\beta}$, standard errors SE($\hat{\beta}$), associated Wald's z-score, and the significance level p for the predictors described above. Positive (negative) coefficients indicate a higher (lower) probability of scrambling. We also report the chi-square value that indicates how much the model is improved by including the predictor. We use the variance inflation factor to assess multicollinearity. Scores range between 1.01 and 1.19, suggesting non-significant influence on the reliability of the parameter estimates (Neter et al., 1996).

Syntactic priming (mean = 0.03, sd = 0.12) fails to achieve significance, primarily because of the distribution of scrambled sentences: only two occur in the same document.[2]

Given-new ordering does not attain significance (subject: mean = 0.42, sd = 0.40, object: mean

[1]The NAIST Text corpus includes coreference annotation, but there are only 8 scrambled objects that are coreference-annotated. On the other hand, there are 92 scrambled objects that include lexically identical mentions (old information).

[2]Including scrambled sentences with topicalized objects (case marker *-wa*) in the analysis did not boost syntactic priming, as only 112 such sentences occur in the corpus.

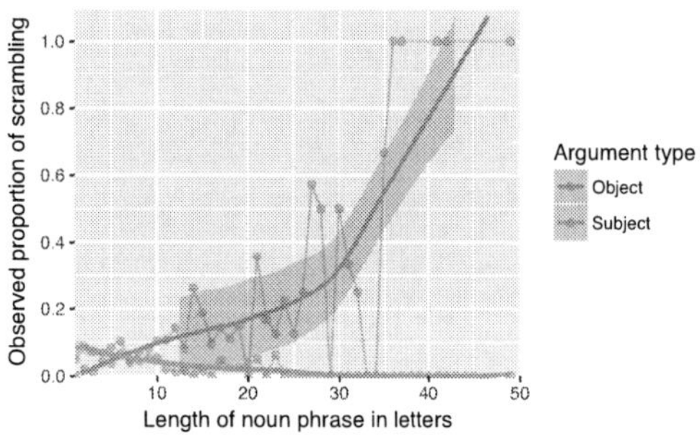

Figure 2: Observed proportion of scrambling by NP length in letters: bold lines are smoothed trend lines with confidence interval around.

= 0.3, sd = 0.38), probably because there is no contrast between scrambled objects and scrambled subjects/canonical objects. [3]

The significant negative correlation with the length of subject NP and the positive correlation with the length of object NP replicate previous studies. The empirical distribution of the proportion of scrambling by the length of subjects and objects in Figure 2 confirms this tendency.

Noun type highly influences the choice of scrambling. A negative correlation of SUBJECT-VERBAL seemingly conflicts with the animacy effect at first glance, but post-hoc examination of the distribution of noun types in Table 2 shows that SUBJECT-VERBAL tends to occur with OBJECT-VERBAL, compared to SUBJECT-FORMAL and SUBJECT-NAME. This suggests there is less inclined to scrambling when both are verbal nouns. SUBJECT-NAME is a significant predictor that correlates negatively with scrambling, showing a strong relation between animate entities and subjects in the canonical position. However, the absence of a positive correlation of OBJECT-NAME indicates the animacy effect is not replicated.

The significant positive correlation of OBJECT-FORMAL suggests that speakers might prefer to place the clausal complement earlier in the sentence. Table 2 shows a higher proportion of scrambling with OBJECT-FORMAL (28 out of 55). Of these 28 scrambled cases, 26 include the clausal objects (71%), whereas 14 of 27 canonical cases include them (51%).

[3] A Welch two-sample t-test: scrambled subjects vs. scrambled objects: $p = 0.66$, canonical objects vs. scrambled objects: $p = 0.33$.

	OBJ-NAME	OBJ-VERBAL	OBJ-FORMAL	OBJ-ELSE	Total
SUBJ-NAME	57 (1)	283 (8)	10 (3)	475 (23)	825 (35)
SUBJ-VERBAL	3 (0)	59 (0)	1 (0)	129 (4)	192 (4)
SUBJ-FORMAL	0 (0)	9 (0)	1 (1)	20 (1)	30 (2)
SUBJ-ELSE	36 (3)	620 (34)	43 (24)	1357 (83)	2056 (144)
Total	96 (4)	971 (42)	55 (28)	1981 (111)	3103 (185)

Table 2: Confusion matrix of noun types: values in the brackets indicate the number of times scrambling occurs.

5 Discussion

We tested multiple factors said to affect scrambling using the naturally distributed data. Although the analysis did not support syntactic priming, given-new ordering, and the animacy effect, we replicated the length effect and established the influence of noun types. These findings only show evidence for sentence-internal factors, but we found no evidence for discourse level factors.

The absence of discourse level effects may be due to the small sample size of scrambled sentences and the low rate of priming in a preceding discourse. It will be important to replicate our results on more extensive data to confirm our observed effects. To scale up the analysis, we will collect a large number of sentences from the web and extract those that are reliably parsed using the method suggested in Sasano and Okumura (2016). The lack of given-new ordering effect is presumably due to our naive procedure for estimating coreferences. For better estimation, future work will involve heuristics known to be robust in Japanese anaphora resolution tasks.

The effect of formal noun implies Japanese speakers' preference for putting the clausal complement earlier (Yamashita and Chang, 2001). The influence of noun type poses a question about what accounts for this *richer content earlier* preference. Future work will explore the potential causes that determine "richness" of the noun phrase.

Acknowledgments

We thank Ryohei Sasano, Tohoku communication science lab semantics group, and four anonymous reviewers for helpful comments and discussion.

References

Mira Ariel. 1990. *Accessing noun-phrase antecedents*. Routledge.

Jennifer E. Arnold, Anthony Losongco, Thomas Wasow, and Ryan Ginstrom. 2000. Heaviness vs. newness: The effects of structural complexity and discourse status on constituent ordering. *Language*, pages 28–55.

Betty J. Birner and Gregory Ward. 2009. Information structure and syntactic structure. *Language and Linguistics Compass*, 3(4):1167–1187.

J. Kathryn Bock and David E. Irwin. 1980. Syntactic effects of information availability in sentence production. *Journal of verbal learning and verbal behavior*, 19(4):467–484.

Victor S. Ferreira and Hiromi Yoshita. 2003. Given-new ordering effects on the production of scrambled sentences in Japanese. *Journal of psycholinguistic research*, 32(6):669–692.

Talmy Givón. 1983. *Topic continuity in discourse: A. quantitative cross-language study*, volume 3. John Benjamins Publishing.

Jeanette K. Gundel, Nancy Hedberg, and Ron Zacharski. 1993. Cognitive status and the form of referring expressions in discourse. *Language*, pages 274–307.

Ryu Iida, Mamoru Komachi, Kentaro Inui, and Yuji Matsumoto. 2007. Annotating a Japanese text corpus with predicate-argument and coreference relations. In *Proceedings of the Linguistic Annotation Workshop*, pages 132–139. Association for Computational Linguistics.

Satoshi Imamura. 2016. A. corpus based analysis of scrambling in Japanese in terms of anaphoric and cataphoric co-referencing. Ms., University of Oxford.

Kazuko Inoue. 1976. *Henkei bunpō to Nihongo (Transformational Grammar and Japanese)*. Taishūkan, New York.

Florian T. Jaeger. 2010. Redundancy and reduction: Speakers manage syntactic information density. *Cognitive psychology*, 61(1):23–62.

Masatoshi Koizumi and Satoshi Imamura. 2016. Interaction between syntactic structure and information structure in the processing of a head-final language. *Journal of psycholinguistic research*, pages 1–14.

Masatoshi Koizumi and Katsuo Tamaoka. 2010. Psycholinguistic evidence for the VP-internal subject position in Japanese. *Linguistic inquiry*, 41(4):663–680.

Kikuo Maekawa, Makoto Yamazaki, Toshinobu Ogiso, Takehiko Maruyama, Hideki Ogura, Wakako Kashino, Hanae Koiso, Masaya Yamaguchi, Makiro Tanaka, and Yasuharu Den. 2014. Balanced corpus of contemporary written Japanese. *Language Resources and Evaluation*, 48(2):345–371.

Shigeru Miyagawa. 1997. Against optional scrambling. *Linguistic inquiry*, pages 1–25.

John Neter, Michael Kutner, William Wasserman, and Christopher Nachtsheim. 1996. *Applied linear regression models*. McGraw-Hill.

Mamoru Saito and Hajime Hoji. 1983. Weak crossover and move α in Japanese. *Natural Language & Linguistic Theory*, 1(2):245–259.

Mamoru Saito. 1985. *Some asymmetries in Japanese and their theoretical implications*. Ph.D. thesis, NA Cambridge.

Ryohei Sasano and Manabu Okumura. 2016. A. corpus-based analysis of canonical word order of Japanese double object constructions. In *Proceedings of the 54th annual meeting on Association for Computational Linguistics*.

Mikihiro N. Tanaka, Holly P. Branigan, Janet F. McLean, and Martin J. Pickering. 2011. Conceptual influences on word order and voice in sentence production: Evidence from Japanese. *Journal of Memory and Language*, 65(3):318–330.

Hiroko Yamashita and Franklin Chang. 2001. "Long before short" preference in the production of a head-final language. *Cognition*, 81(2):B45–B55.

Hiroko Yamashita, Franklin Chang, and Yuki Hirose. 2002. Separating functions and positions: Evidence from structural priming in Japanese. In *15th CUNY Conference on Human Sentence Processing*.

Hiroko Yamashita. 2002. Scrambled sentences in Japanese: Linguistic properties and motivations for production. *TEXT & Talk: An Interdisciplinary Journal of Language, Discourse & Communication Studies*, 22(4):597–634.

Association for Computational Linguistics
209 N. Eighth Street
Stroudsburg, Pennsylvania 18360

CURRAN ASSOCIATES INC.
proceedings
.com

ISBN 978-1-5108-3861-1

9 781510 838611